Simply Shakespeare

Original Shakespearean Text
With a Modern Line-for-Line Translation

THE TEMPEST

BARRON'S

All inquiries should be addressed to:
Barron's Educational Series, Inc.
250 Wireless Boulevard
Hauppauge, New York 11788
http://www.barronseduc.com

ISBN-13: 978-0-7641-2087-9
ISBN-10: 0-7641-2087-5

Library of Congress Catalog Card No. 2001043311

Library of Congress Cataloging-in-Publication Data

Shakespeare, William, 1564–1616.
    The tempest / edited and rendered into modern English by Kathleen M. Ermitage.
        p. cm. — (Simply Shakespeare)
    Includes bibliographical references.
    Summary: Presents the original text of Shakespeare's play side by side with a modern version, with discussion questions, role-playing scenarios, and other study activities.
    ISBN 0-7641-2087-5
        1. Survival after airplane accidents, shipwrecks, etc.—Juvenile drama.
    2. Fathers and daughters--Juvenile drama. 3. Castaways—Juvenile drama.
    4. Magicians—Juvenile drama. 5. Children's plays, English. [1. Shakespeare, William, 1564–1616. Tempest. 2. Plays. 3. English literature—History and criticism.] I. Ermitage, Kathleen. II. Title.

PR2833 .A25 2002
822.3'3—dc21
                                                                    2001043311

PRINTED IN CHINA
9 8 7 6

Simply Shakespeare

Titles in the Series

Contents

Introduction

William Shakespeare, 1564–1616

Who was William Shakespeare? This simple question has challenged scholars for years. The man behind vivid, unforgettable characters like Hamlet, Romeo and Juliet, and King Lear is a shadow compared to his creations. Luckily, official records of Shakespeare's time have preserved some facts about his life.

Shakespeare was born in April 1564 in Stratford-upon-Avon, England. His father, John Shakespeare, was a prominent local merchant. Shakespeare probably attended grammar school in Stratford, learning basic Latin and Greek and studying works by ancient Roman writers. In 1582, when Shakespeare was 18, he married Anne Hathaway. Eventually, the couple had three children—but, like many families in their day, they were forced to endure a tragic loss when Hamnet, their only son, died at age 11.

No records document Shakespeare's life from 1585 to 1592, when he was between the ages of 21 and 28. In his writings, Shakespeare seems to know so much about so many things that it's tempting to make guesses about how he supported his young family during this period. Over the years, it's been speculated that he worked as a schoolteacher, a butcher, or an actor—and even that he did a little poaching as a young man. Thanks to some London theater gossip left behind by a professional rival, we know that Shakespeare was living in London as a playwright and an actor by 1592. Meanwhile, Anne and the children stayed in Stratford.

This must have been a thrilling time for Shakespeare. In 1592, England was becoming a powerful nation under its great and clever queen, Elizabeth I. English explorers and colonists crossed seas to search strange new worlds. London was a bustling, exciting center of commerce, full of travelers from abroad. And though many Europeans still looked down on English culture, they admitted that London's stages boasted some of the best plays and actors to be found. Travelers from all over admired the dramas of Christopher Marlowe, Thomas Kyd, and the new name on the scene, William Shakespeare.

Nevertheless, the life of the theater had its hazards. London's actors, playwrights, and theatrical entrepreneurs chose a risky and somewhat shady line of work. Religious leaders condemned the theater for encouraging immorality and idleness among the London populace. London's city leaders, fearful of crowds, closed the theaters in times of unrest or plague. Luckily, the London troupes had some powerful "fans"—members of the nobility who acted as patrons, protecting the troupes from their enemies. Queen Elizabeth herself loved plays. Special performances were regularly given for her at court.

By 1594, two theatrical companies had emerged as the most popular. Archrivals, The Lord Admiral's Men and The Lord Chamberlain's Men performed at the Rose and the Theatre, respectively. However, The Lord Chamberlain's Men had an ace: Shakespeare was both a founding member and the company's main playwright. The company's fine lead actor was Richard Burbage, the first man to play such roles as Hamlet, Othello, and Macbeth. With a one-two punch like that, it's not surprising that The Lord Chamberlain's Men soon emerged as London's top troupe. By 1597, Shakespeare had written such works as *Romeo and Juliet, The Merchant of Venice,* and *A Midsummer Night's Dream.* His finances grew with his reputation, and he was able to buy land and Stratford's second-largest house, where Anne and the children moved while he remained in London.

Then as now, owning property went a long way. Like many acting companies to this day, The Lord Chamberlain's Men got involved in a bitter dispute with their landlord. However, they owned the actual timbers of the Theatre building—which turned out to be useful assets. Eventually the exasperated troupe hired a builder to secretly take apart the Theatre, then transported its timbers across London to the south bank of the River Thames. There, they used the Theatre's remains to construct their new home—The Globe.

At The Globe, many of Shakespeare's greatest plays first came to life. From 1599 until his death in 1616, the open-air Globe served as Shakespeare's main stage. Audiences saw the first performances of *Hamlet, Macbeth, Twelfth Night,* and *King Lear* there. (In winter, Shakespeare's company performed at London's Blackfriars, the indoor theater that housed the first performance of *The Tempest.*) In 1603, after the death of Queen Elizabeth, Shakespeare's troupe added a new triumph to its résumé. Changing its name to The King's Men, it became the official theatrical company of England's new monarch, James I. The company performed frequently at court and state functions for its powerful new patron.

Around 1611–1612, Shakespeare returned permanently to Stratford. Unfortunately, we know little about his domestic life there. Where Shakespeare is concerned, there's no "tell-all" biography to reveal his intimate life. Was he happily wed to Anne, or did he live for so long in London to escape a bad marriage? Do the sonnets Shakespeare published in 1609 tell us a real-life story of his relationships with a young man, a "Dark Lady," and a rival for the lady's love? What were Shakespeare's political beliefs? From his writings, it's clear that Shakespeare understood life's best and worst emotions very deeply. But we'll never know how much of his own life made its way into his art. He died at the age of 53 on April 23, 1616, leaving behind the almost 40 plays and scores of poems that have spoken for him to generations of readers and listeners. Shakespeare is buried in Holy Trinity Church in Stratford, where he lies under a stone that warns the living—in verse—never to disturb his bones.

Shakespeare's Theater

Going to a play in Shakespeare's time was a completely different experience than going to a play today. How theaters were built, who attended, what happened during the performance, and who produced the plays were all quite unlike most theater performances today.

Theaters in Shakespeare's time were mainly outside the walls of the city of London—and away from the authorities *in* London. In those times, many religious authorities (especially radical Protestants) condemned plays and playgoing. They preached that plays, being stage illusions, were acts of deception and therefore sinful. The city authorities in London agreed that the theaters encouraged immorality. Despite this, theaters did exist in and around the city of London. They were, however, housed in neighborhoods known as Liberties. Liberties were areas that previously had religious functions and therefore were under the control of the crown, not the city of London. Luckily for playgoers, the monarchs Elizabeth and James were more tolerant of the amusements offered by the stage than the London authorities.

Who enjoyed what the stage had to offer? Almost all of London society went to the theater. Merchants and their wives, prostitutes, lawyers, laborers, and visitors from other countries would attend. Once you were at the theater, your social station dictated what you could pay and where you sat. If you could only afford a pence (about a penny), you would stand in the yard immediately surrounding the stage.

(These members of Shakespeare's audience were called "groundlings.") As many as a thousand other spectators might join you there. In the yard everyone would be exposed to the weather and to peddlers selling fruit and nuts. Your experience would probably be more active and less quiet than attending a play today. Movement was not uncommon. If you wanted a better or different view, you might rove about the yard. If you paid another pence, you could move into a lower gallery.

The galleries above and surrounding the stage on all sides could accommodate up to 2,000 more people. However, because the galleries were vertical and surrounded the stage, no matter where you sat, you would never be more than 35 feet away from the stage. The galleries immediately behind the stage were reserved for members of the nobility and royalty. From behind the stage a noble could not only see everything, but—more importantly—could be seen by others in the audience! Queen Elizabeth and King James were less likely to attend a theater performance, although they protected theater companies. Instead, companies performed plays for them at court.

The Globe's stage was similar to the other outdoor theaters in Shakespeare's time. These stages offered little decoration or frills. Consequently, the actors and the text carried the burden of delivering the drama. Without the help of scenery or lighting, the audience had to imagine what was not represented on the stage (the storms, shipwrecks, and so forth). The Globe's stage was rectangular—with dimensions of about 27 by 44 feet. At the back of the stage was a curtained wall containing three entrances onto the stage. These entrances led directly from the tiring (as in "attiring") house, where the actors would dress. The middle entrance was covered by a hanging tapestry and was probably used for special entrances—such as a ceremonial procession or the delivery of a prologue.

Unlike the yard, the stage was covered by a canopied roof that was suspended by two columns. This canopy was known as the *heavens*. Its underside was covered with paintings of the sun, moon, stars, and sky and was visible to all theatergoers. *Hell* was the area below the stage with a trapdoor as the entrance. Immediately behind and one flight above the stage were the dressing rooms, and above them lay the storage area for props and costumes.

Indoor theaters were similar to outdoor theaters in many respects. They featured a bare stage with the heavens, a trapdoor leading to hell, and doors leading to the tiring house. Builders created indoor theaters from preexisting space in already constructed buildings. These theaters were smaller, and because they were in town they were also more expensive. Standing in the yard of an outdoor theater cost a pence. The cheapest seat in an *indoor* theater was sixpence. The most fashionable and wealthy members of London society attended indoor theaters as much to see as to be seen. If you were a gallant (a fashionable theatergoer), you could pay 24 pence and actually sit on a stool at the edge of the stage—where everyone could see you.

The actors' costumes were also on display. Whether plays were performed indoors or outdoors, costumes were richly decorated. They were one of the main assets of a theater company and one of the draws of theater. However, costumes didn't necessarily match the period of the play's setting. How spectacular the costumes looked was more important than how realistic they were or if they matched the period setting.

These costumes were worn on stage only by men or boys who were a part of licensed theater companies. The actors in the companies were exclusively male and frequently doubled up on parts. Boys played female roles before their voices changed. Some actors were also shareholders—the most important members of a theater company. The shareholders owned the company's assets (the play texts, costumes, and props) and made a profit from the admissions gathered. Besides the shareholders and those actors who did not hold shares, other company members were apprentices and hired men and musicians.

The actors in Shakespeare's day worked hard. They were paid according to the house's take. New plays were staged rapidly, possibly with as little as three weeks from the time a company first received the play text until opening night. All the while, the companies appeared to have juggled a large number of new and older plays in performance. In lead roles, the most popular actors might have delivered as many as 4,000 lines in six different plays during a London working week! Working at this pace, it seems likely that teamwork was key to a company's success.

The Sound of Shakespeare

Shakespeare's heroes and heroines all share one quality: They're all great talkers. They combine Shakespeare's powerful imagery and vocabulary with a sound that thunders, trills, rocks, and sings.

When Shakespearean actors say their lines, they don't just speak lines of dialogue. Often, they're also speaking lines of dramatic poetry that are written in a sound pattern called *iambic pentameter*. When these lines don't rhyme and are not grouped in stanzas, they're called *blank verse*. Though many passages in Shakespeare plays are written in prose, the most important and serious moments are almost always in iambic pentameter. As Shakespeare matured, the sound of his lines began to change. Late plays like *The Tempest* are primarily in a wonderfully flowing blank verse. Earlier works, such as *Romeo and Juliet*, feature much more rhymed iambic pentameter, often with punctuation at the end of each line to make the rhymes even stronger.

Terms like "iambic pentameter" sound scarily technical—like part of a chemistry experiment that will blow up the building if you measure it wrong. But the Greeks, who invented iambic pentameter, used it as a dance beat. Later writers no longer used it as something one could literally shimmy to, but it was still a way to organize the rhythmic noise and swing of speech. An *iamb* contains one unaccented (or unstressed) syllable and one accented (stressed) syllable, in that order. It borrows from the natural swing of our heartbeats to go *ker-THUMP, ker-THUMP*. Five of these ker-thumping units in a row make a line of iambic *penta*meter.

Dance or rock music needs a good, regular thumping of drums (or drum machine) and bass to get our feet tapping and bodies dancing, but things can get awfully monotonous if that's all there is to the sound. Poetry works the same way. With its ten syllables and five ker-thumps, a line like "he WENT to TOWN toDAY to BUY a CAR" is perfect iambic pentameter. It's just as regular as a metronome. But it isn't poetry. "In SOOTH/ I KNOW/ not WHY/ I AM/ so SAD" is poetry (*The Merchant of Venice*, Act 1, Scene 1). Writers like Shakespeare change the iambic pentameter pattern of their blank verse all the time to keep things sounding interesting. The melody of vowels and other sound effects makes the lines even more musical and varied. As it reaches the audience's ears, this mix of basic, patterned beat and sound variations carries powerful messages of meaning and emotion. The beating, regular rhythms of blank verse also help actors remember their lines.

Why did Shakespeare use this form? Blank verse dominated through a combination of novelty, tradition, and ease. The Greeks and Romans passed on a tradition of combining poetry and drama. English playwrights experimented with this tradition by using all sorts of verse and prose for their plays. By the 1590s, blank verse had caught on with some of the best new writers in London. In the hands of writers like the popular Christopher Marlowe and the up-and-coming Will Shakespeare, it was more than just the latest craze in on-stage sound.

Blank verse also fit well with the English language itself. Compared to languages like French and Italian, English is hard to rhyme. It's also heavily accentual—another way of saying that English really bumps and thumps.

The words and sounds coming from the stage were new and thrilling to Shakespeare's audience. England was falling in love with its own language. English speakers were still making up grammar, spelling, and pronunciation as they went along—giving the language more of a "hands-on" feel than it has today. The grammar books and dictionaries that finally fixed the "rules" of English did not appear until after Shakespeare's death. The language grew and grew, soaking up words from other languages, combining and making new words. Politically, the country also grew in power and pride.

Shakespeare's language reflects this sense of freedom, experimentation, and power. When he put his words in the beat of blank verse and the mouths of London's best actors, it must have sounded a little like the birth of rock and roll—mixing old styles and new sounds to make a new, triumphant swagger.

Publishing Shakespeare

Books of Shakespeare's plays come in all shapes and sizes. They range from slim paperbacks like this one to heavy, muscle-building anthologies of his collected works. Libraries devote shelves of space to works by and about "the Bard." Despite all that paper and ink, no printed text of a Shakespeare play can claim to be an exact, word-by-word copy of what Shakespeare wrote.

Today, most writers work on computers and can save their work electronically. Students everywhere know the horror of losing the only copy of something they've written and make sure they always have a backup version! In Shakespeare's time, a playwright delivered a handwritten copy of his work to the acting company that asked him to write a play. This may have been his only copy—which was now the property of the company, not the writer. In general, plays were viewed as mere "entertainments"—not literary art. They were written quickly and were often disposed of when the acting companies had no more use for them.

The draft Shakespeare delivered was a work in progress. He and the company probably added, deleted, and changed some material—stage directions, entrances and exits, even lines and character names—during rehearsals. Companies may have had a clean copy written out by a scribe (a professional hand-writer) or by the writer himself. Most likely they kept this house copy for future performances. No copies of Shakespeare's plays in his own handwriting have survived.

Acting companies might perform a hit play for years before it was printed, usually in small books called *quartos*. However, the first published versions of Shakespeare's plays vary considerably. Some of these texts are thought to be of an inferior, incomplete quality. Because of this, scholars have speculated that they are not based on authoritative, written copies, but were re-created from actors' memories or from the shorthand notes of a scribe working for a publisher.

Shakespearean scholars often call these apparently faulty versions of his plays "bad quartos." Why might such texts have appeared? Scholars have guessed that they are "pirated versions." They believe that acting companies tried to keep their plays out of print to prevent rival troupes from stealing popular material. However, booksellers sometimes printed unauthorized versions of Shakespeare's plays that were used by competing companies. The pirated versions may have been done with help from actors who had played minor roles in the play, memorized it, and then sold their unreliable, memorized versions. (In recent years, this theory has been challenged by some scholars who argue that the "bad" quartos may be based on Shakespeare's own first drafts or that they reliably reflect early performance texts of the plays.)

"Good" quartos were printed with the permission of the company that owned the play and were based on written copies. However, even these authorized versions were far from perfect. The printers had to work either by deciphering the playwright's handwriting or by using a flawed version printed earlier. They also had to memorize lines as they manually set type on the press. And they decided how a line should be punctuated and spelled—not always with foolproof judgment!

The first full collection of Shakespeare's plays came out in 1623, seven years after his death. Called the "First Folio," this collection included 36 plays compiled by John Heminge and Henry Condell, actor-friends of Shakespeare from The King's Men troupe.

To develop the First Folio texts, Heminge, Condell, and their co-editors probably worked with a mix of handwritten and both good and bad printed versions of their friend's plays. Their 1623 version had many errors, and though later editions of that text corrected some mistakes, they also added new ones. The First Folio also contained no indications of where acts and scenes began and ended. The scene and act divisions that appear standard in most modern editions of Shakespeare actually rely on the shrewd guesses of generations of editors and researchers.

Most modern editors of Shakespeare depend on a combination of trustworthy early publications to come up with the most accurate text possible. They often use the versions in the First Folio, its later editions, and other "good," authorized publications of single plays. In some cases, they also consult "bad" versions or rely on pure guesswork to decide the most likely reading of some words or lines. Because of such uncertainties, modern editions of Shakespeare often vary, depending on editors' research and choices. This version of William Shakespeare's *The Tempest* is taken from the Folio Edition of 1623.

The Tempest

Introduction to the Play

Nearly four hundred years ago, William Shakespeare cast a most powerful spell. He created *The Tempest*—a mysterious, moody drama that still enchants audiences. Amazing sights and powerful poetry fill this play, which is dominated by a main character with magic powers. But *The Tempest*'s best magic act is its effect on audiences and readers. After Prospero, the main character, has spoken the play's final lines and the applause begins, the play's powerful mood lingers, much like the feeling when one awakens from a dream or an enchantment. What has just occurred? And what did it mean?

The first question is easier to answer. *The Tempest* has a bare-bones plot. And since much of the action proceeds according to Prospero's plans and takes place under his watchful eye, there's little suspense. In place of a more complex development of plot, Shakespeare provides wonderful sights and sounds. *The Tempest* is full of music, magical spirits, and transformations. There's even a kind of mini-play (called a *masque*) performed by magical actors, who take on the roles of Roman goddesses. Spectacular action marks the play from its very first scene, in which sailors battle the terrible tempest (storm) of the play's title.

How might one interpret such action? When audiences try to pin down just one meaning, *The Tempest* often slips out of their grasps. The play lends itself to numerous readings, and scholars and theatrical productions have interpreted it in many different ways. Often, an interpretation depends on a particular view of certain characters, especially Prospero, Caliban, and Ariel. Some argue that the play shows the triumph of art (represented by Prospero, aided by Ariel) over nature (Caliban). For others, it represents a debate on the merits of civilization versus a life closely tied to the natural world. And some modern-day productions present *The Tempest* as an anticolonialist tale. In this view, Caliban is reminiscent of the native populations in the New World—a longtime resident of the island who is exploited by the European newcomers. As is so often the case in Shakespeare's works, *The Tempest* speaks in different ways to different individuals, generations, and eras. Nevertheless, it continues to speak in unexpected and powerful ways.

It is fitting that interpretations of *The Tempest* change, because change itself is a major theme of the play. Prospero's magic relies on amazing transformations (as when Ariel changes into fire or the spirits transform into goddesses or dogs). Some of the play's most famous lines speak of life's fleeting, changeable qualities. As Prospero tells us, "We [humans] are such stuff / As dreams are made on" (Act 4, Scene 1, lines 170–171), while Ariel's song about a drowned man notes that his body "suffer[s] / A sea change." The play's ending stresses repentance and forgiveness—emotions that rely on a change of heart. By the play's end, one of the best ways to rate which of *The Tempest*'s characters may be "good" or "bad" is to observe their ability to change. Who has simply "suffered" change, and who changes and learns from what they have experienced?

Most scholars think *The Tempest* was written between late 1610 and late 1611. These dates are partly based on the time line suggested by Shakespeare's sources (see the "Sources" section) and partly on the style of the play's flowing blank verse (see "The Sound of Shakespeare"). Also, *The Tempest* seems closely allied with other plays that Shakespeare probably wrote late in his career. These include *Pericles*, *Cymbeline*, and *The Winter's Tale*. Like *The Tempest*, all take a lighter, gentler tone than Shakespeare's dark and sorrowful last tragedies.

However, the four lighter plays are not exactly comedies. Often described as "tragicomic," they are known as Shakespeare's *romances*. Magic, miracles, and exotic locations link them. So do ideas of reconciliation, forgiveness, and bitter hardships that turn fruitful in the end. The characters' suffering sometimes lends the romances a moody, bittersweet note—especially in *The Tempest*.

The four romances share another characteristic: They focus on the relationship between fathers and daughters—a frequent theme in Shakespeare. Some argue that as Shakespeare contemplated retirement, his thoughts were with his own daughters from whom he was separated for long periods during his career. In these plays the father is frequently reconciled with the daughter from whom he has been separated, just as Shakespeare himself was reconciled with his daughters.

The Tempest was probably the last play written entirely by Shakespeare, so many readers have been tempted to view Prospero's final speech and his farewell to his art as Shakespeare's own backward glance at his life in the theater. Whether or not Shakespeare really had such a meaning in mind will remain one of *The Tempest*'s many mysteries. Still, the idea fits well with the play's sad yet sweet, stormy yet contained, and dreamy but lasting mood. This strange last play stands as one of Shakespeare's most powerful and best-loved works.

The Tempest's Sources

Most of *The Tempest*'s characters essentially drifted to the island and washed up on its shores. When Shakespeare wrote his plays, he too must have been a collector of drifting items. We can never know exactly what emotions drove this great genius to write, but it seems clear that he found material everywhere. And it *came* to him from everywhere. Old news and current events, folklore and science, politics, philosophy, mythology, and ancient literature all found their ways into his plays. There, they were unified with astonishing ease.

The Tempest differs from many Shakespeare plays (*Romeo and Juliet*, for example) in that Shakespeare probably invented its plot himself, rather than borrowing the story's basics from another source. While elements of the play's plot are echoed in other European literature and drama, most of these works only seem to show how Shakespeare's play makes inventive use of some stock situations and character types in folklore and literary romance.

Scholars have suggested many sources that influenced parts of the play's action, theme, and dialogue. In 1610, reports reached England about the experiences of a group of colonists bound for Virginia. Their ship was blown off course by a hurricane and ran aground in the Bermuda islands. Sailors had believed that this place was inhabited by devils, but the stranded colonists discovered its beauty and abundance, even as they contended with a mutiny among their group. Eventually they arrived safely in Virginia.

One colonist, William Strachey, wrote a letter describing his adventures. It was published in 1625 as *A True Reportory of the Wracke and Redemption of Sir Thomas Gates, Knight,* but it circulated in manuscript much earlier and it seems likely that Shakespeare saw it. (He may even have known the writer.) Strachey's text provided a basis for much of Shakespeare's description of *The Tempest*'s storm and shipwreck, as well as some of the castaways' reactions to the island and the significant role of Providence in their salvation. It seems likely that Shakespeare may have also drawn on other reports of the same shipwreck, such as Sylvester Jourdain's *The Discovery of the Bermudas* (1610).

Gonzalo's description of an ideal society in Act 2 (Scene 1, lines 154–163, 167–172) also borrows from writings about the New World.

Here, Shakespeare's source was the French philosopher Michel de Montaigne. Montaigne had read reports of the indigenous societies that Europeans found when they arrived in the Americas. His essay stresses his impressions of their simple, natural, innocent way of life and opposes it to corrupt European civilization. Some of Montaigne's sentiments and words are echoed in Gonzalo's speech.

Echoes from a different source may be heard in the voice of Prospero. Near the beginning of Act 5, he gives a speech that recalls a passage from *Metamorphoses* by the Roman poet Ovid. Ovid's book is a long poem that retells the stories behind many Greek and Roman myths. One passage contains a monologue by Medea, a legendary sorceress, and seems to have inspired some of the language in Prospero's speech bidding farewell to his magic powers (lines 38–62). Shakespeare may have had the overall spirit of *Metamorphoses* in mind as he wrote *The Tempest*, for both works are filled with wondrous transformations and images from a natural world full of variety and change.

Prospero's final speech may have another layer of significance. If Shakespeare did intend *The Tempest* to be his last play, then the metaphor of *life* as a journey in which we encounter calm seas and rough seas—smooth sailing and tempests—and in which we hope to arrive at a "reasonable shore," in Gonzalo's words, makes the play even more poignant in light of Shakespeare's retirement from the theater and his return to his own "reasonable shore" in Stratford.

The Text of *The Tempest*

The first published version of *The Tempest* appeared in the First Folio (see "Publishing Shakespeare") in 1623. It is the first play in the volume, and it appears to have been carefully prepared and transcribed from a King's Men's copy. This version of *The Tempest* also contains a fairly large number of elaborate stage directions, which is unusual in Shakespeare's plays. Scholars aren't certain whether the directions were provided by Shakespeare himself or by a later hand, but since the First Folio text is the earliest known published version of the play, all modern-day editions rely on it as their primary, authoritative text.

The first documented performance of *The Tempest* took place at court, as a special performance before King James on November 1, 1611. It is generally believed that this was not the play's actual premiere. However, scholars have also guessed that Shakespeare could not have written the play any earlier than late 1610, because some of his likely sources would not have been available until then.

The Tempest

Original text and modern version

Characters

Alonso   the king of Naples

Sebastian   Alonso's brother

Prospero   the rightful duke of Milan

Antonio   his brother, who usurped his title

Ferdinand   the king of Naples's son

Gonzalo   an honest old counsellor to Alonso

Adrian
Francisco } lords who serve Alonso

Caliban   a deformed creature who is Prospero's slave

Trinculo   a clown

Stephano   a drunken butler

Ship's master

Boatswain

Sailors

Miranda   Prospero's daughter

Ariel   a spirit of the air

Iris
Ceres
Juno } spirits
Nymphs
Reapers

All the World's a Stage Introduction

Out on the ocean, a wild storm batters a stately ship. Despite the crew's desperate efforts, the ship sinks. One by one, several survivors find their ways to a nearby island's shores. They look around on its empty beaches. Are there footprints in the sand? Who lives here?

With *The Tempest* (c. 1611), Shakespeare took his audiences to strange new territory. Late in his life, he began to experiment with a new kind of play—creating magical, dreamy, bittersweet works that didn't quite fit the old categories. *The Tempest* is the best-known of these plays, which are often called *romances*. For Shakespeare's actors and audience, the bare stage of these romances was also a wonderful new shore.

What's in a Name? Characters

What characters journey to this shore? In Act 1 we meet Prospero, who stands at the center of the play. He and his daughter, Miranda, came to the island from Italy, where he was once Duke of Milan. Prospero knows magic and can control the island's supernatural spirits, including an airy creature named Ariel. Prospero also commands a slave, Caliban, who was born on the island.

Using his magic, Prospero can now take revenge against his brother, Antonio, and Alonso, the King of Naples. Previously, Alonso and Antonio had plotted together against Prospero. Prospero's plans for revenge also include Ferdinand, Alonso's beloved son, as well as a kind counselor named Gonzalo.

COME WHAT MAY Things to Watch For

The Tempest is full of attractive pictures of Prospero's island. Shakespeare writes with all his senses to make lovely poetry about the natural world. To some audiences today, the island might sound at first like an unspoiled paradise.

Does living in unspoiled nature make a person good? Throughout *The Tempest,* watch for how Shakespeare explores this question. The natural world is both generous and harsh in the play—mild and dreamy, stormy and cruel, as is human nature. Shakespeare gathers together some highly civilized visitors to the island with one savage who was born there—Caliban. The mix creates some surprises for the audience. You may find yourself rooting for wild Caliban at one point and for an Italian nobleman at the next.

All Our Yesterdays Historical and Social Context

Land ho! London was filled with exciting news from overseas during Shakespeare's time. The English had become colonizers, with settlements across the Atlantic Ocean.

In 1609, the English ship *Sea Venture* was blown off course by a hurricane and shipwrecked on Bermuda, stranding 150 travelers. Some of the castaways wrote about their experiences, describing their delight at the island's beauty and their fears that it was inhabited by devils. Shakespeare also seems to have known about the adventures of English travelers and settlers in Virginia.

Europeans sometimes *civilized* these paradises—tried to make them conform to life as the Europeans thought it should be—in violent ways. Slavery was a common practice. Native peoples were pushed out and often murdered. *The Tempest* seems to hint at these disasters. Many modern-day stagings of the play treat it as a story that is partly about colonialism and racism. We don't know what Shakespeare thought about these issues. We *do* know he had an amazing understanding of how people used and misused power.

The Play's the Thing Staging

Many of Shakespeare's plays were first performed at the Globe, an outdoor theater. Common folks and highborn types mixed at the Globe. Scholars think that they were a mobile and fairly noisy crowd.

The Tempest was probably written for performance at an indoor theater, called the Blackfriars. The Blackfriars catered to a more sophisticated audience that could afford higher ticket prices. Its stage was smaller and its audiences sat and watched in a candlelit hall. Plays there reflected this setting. Playwrights used fewer actors on stage and cut back on some of the fireworks and fights used on outdoor stages. Music, magical effects, and witty language took up the slack.

My Words Fly Up Language

Throughout *The Tempest*, Prospero refers to his art, so we think of him as a painter or a poet. At times, *art* simply means learning or science, as when Prospero speaks of the "liberal Arts." But Prospero is actually referring to the art of magic. As the play begins, Prospero uses his art to shape and control the natural world, to arrange things the way he wants them. How close is this to the type of art that writers like Shakespeare create?

One of Shakespeare's favorite adjectives in *The Tempest* is *brave*. For him, *brave* could mean "splendid" or "wonderful," as it frequently does in *The Tempest*. *Brave* could also mean "courageous," as it does today. In Act 1, Shakespeare uses *brave* in this more familiar way when Ferdinand refers to Antonio's "brave son."

Act I

Scene I

A ship at sea: a tempestuous noise of thunder and lightning is heard

[*Enter a* **Ship-master** *and a* **Boatswain**]

Master Boatswain!

Boatswain Here, master; what cheer?

Master Good, speak to the mariners; fall to 't, yarely, or we run ourselves aground; bestir, bestir.

[*Exit*]

[*Enter* **Mariners**]

5 **Boatswain** Heigh, my hearts! Cheerly, cheerly, my hearts! Yare, yare! Take in the topsail. Tend to th' master's whistle. Blow till thou burst thy wind, if room enough!

[*Enter* **Alonso, Sebastian, Antonio, Ferdinand, Gonzalo,** *and others*]

Alonso Good boatswain, have care. Where's the master? Play the men.

10 **Boatswain** I pray now, keep below.

A ship at sea. A storm with thunder and lightning. A **Captain** *and* **Boatswain** *enter.*

Captain Boatswain!

Boatswain Here, Captain! What is it?

Captain Call all hands! Get to it, smartly, or we'll run ourselves aground! Quickly! Quickly!

[**Captain** *exits*]

[**Sailors** *enter*]

Boatswain Heave, my hearties! Harder! Harder, my hearties! Smartly, smartly! Take in the topsail. Mind the captain's whistle. [*Addressing the storm*] Blow until you burst your lungs, so long as we've space to maneuver!

[**Alonso, Sebastian, Antonio, Ferdinand, Gonzalo,** *and others enter*]

Alonso Good boatswain, be careful. Where's the captain? Urge on the men.

Boatswain Please now, stay below.

Antonio Where is the master, boatswain?

Boatswain Do you not hear him? You mar our labour; keep
your cabins; you do assist the storm.

Gonzalo Nay, good, be patient.

15 **Boatswain** When the sea is. Hence! What cares these roarers
for the name of King? To cabin: silence! Trouble us not.

Gonzalo Good, yet remember whom thou hast aboard.

Boatswain None that I more love than myself. You are a
counsellor; if you can command these elements to silence,
20 and work the peace of the present, we will not hand a rope
more; use your authority; if you cannot, give thanks you have
lived so long, and make yourself ready in your cabin for the
mischance of the hour, if it so hap. Cheerly, good hearts!
Out of our way, I say.

[*Exit*]

25 **Gonzalo** I have great comfort from this fellow; methinks he
hath no drowning mark upon him; his complexion is perfect
gallows. Stand fast, good Fate, to his hanging. Make the
rope of his destiny our cable, for our own doth little
advantage. If he be not born to be hanged, our case is
30 miserable.

[*Exeunt*]

[*Enter* **Boatswain**]

Antonio Where's the captain, boatswain?

Boatswain Don't you hear him? You're getting in our way. Stay in your cabins. You're helping the storm.

Gonzalo Now, good fellow, be patient.

Boatswain Not until the sea is patient! Go! What do these roarers care about a king? Go to your cabin and be quiet! Don't bother us!

Gonzalo Good man, remember whom you have aboard!

Boatswain No one that I love more than myself. You're a member of the King's council. If you can command these elements to be silent and make the seas peaceful, we won't haul more rope. Use your authority. If you can't, then be thankful you've lived so long, and prepare yourself in your cabin for an unlucky event, if it happens. Harder, my hearties! Out of our way, I say!

[**Boatswain** *exits*]

Gonzalo I get great comfort from this fellow. I don't think he's been marked for drowning. He has the appearance of someone who's meant to be hanged on the gallows. Well, Fate, stick to his hanging. Make the rope that will hang him our anchor chain, since the one we have does us little good. If he's not born to be hanged, then our situation is very bad.

[*They exit*]

[*The* **Boatswain** *enters*]

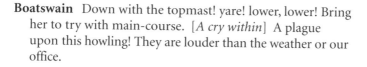

Boatswain Down with the topmast! yare! lower, lower! Bring her to try with main-course. [*A cry within*] A plague upon this howling! They are louder than the weather or our office.

[*Enter* **Sebastian, Antonio** *and* **Gonzalo**]

35   Yet again! What do you here? Shall we give o'er, and drown? Have you a mind to sink?

Sebastian A pox o' your throat, you bawling, blasphemous, incharitable dog!

Boatswain Work you then?

40 **Antonio** Hang, cur! hang, you whoreson, insolent noise-maker. We are less afraid to be drowned than thou art.

Gonzalo I'll warrant him for drowning, though the ship were no stronger than a nutshell, and as leaky as an unstanched wench.

45 **Boatswain** Lay her a-hold, a-hold! set her two courses; off to sea again; lay her off.

[*Enter* **Mariners,** *wet*]

Mariners All lost, to prayers, to prayers! All lost!

[*Exeunt*]

Boatswain What, must our mouths be cold?

Gonzalo The King and Prince at prayers, let's assist them,
50   For our case is as theirs.

Sebastian   I'm out of patience.

Antonio We are merely cheated of our lives by drunkards:
This wide-chapped rascal – would thou mightst lie drowning
The washing of ten tides!

Boatswain Down with the topmast! Smartly! Lower, lower! Keep her close to the wind with the mainsail. [*Shouting off-stage*] A plague upon this howling! They're louder than the weather or our working!

[**Sebastian, Antonio,** *and* **Gonzalo** *enter*]

Again? What do you want here? Shall we give up and drown? Do you want to sink?

Sebastian A plague on your throat, you bawling, blasphemous, uncharitable dog!

Boatswain Are you going to work, then?

Antonio Hang, you dog! Hang, you insolent, illegitimate loudmouth. We're less afraid to be drowned than you are!

Gonzalo I'll guarantee him against drowning, even if the ship were no stronger than a nutshell and as leaky as an incontinent woman.

Boatswain Lay her hull to the wind! Set her mainsail and foresail, out to sea again! Turn her!

[**Sailors** *enter, soaking wet*]

Sailors We're lost! Start praying, start praying! We're lost!

[**Sailors** *exit*]

Boatswain Well, must our mouths be deadly cold?

Gonzalo The King and Prince are at prayers. Let's go to them. Our situation is the same as theirs.

Sebastian I've run out of patience!

Antonio We're simply cheated of our lives by drunkards! That big mouthed rascal. [*Referring to the* **Boatswain**] I hope you do drown, and you're washed over by ten tides!

55 **Gonzalo**   He'll be hanged yet,
   Though every drop of water swear against it,
   And gape at widest to glut him.

   [*A confused noise within*] 'Mercy on us!' –'We split, we
   split!' – 'Farewell, my wife and children!' – 'Farewell,
60 brother!' – 'We split, we split, we split!'

Antonio Let's all sink wi' th' King.

Sebastian Let's take leave of him.

                [*Exeunt* **Antonio** *and* **Sebastian**]

Gonzalo Now would I give a thousand furlongs of sea for an
   acre of barren ground, long heath, broom, furze, anything.
65 The wills above be done! But I would fain die a dry death.

                            [*Exeunt*]

Gonzalo He'll be hanged someday, even though every drop of water swears I'm wrong, and the sea opens to its widest to swallow him.

[*Noises of panic are heard*] "Have mercy on us!" — "We're splitting apart, we're splitting apart!" — "Farewell my wife and children!" — "Farewell, brothers!" — "We're splitting apart, we're splitting, we're splitting!"

Antonio Let's all sink with the King.

Sebastian Let's say our good-byes to him.

[**Antonio** *and* **Sebastian** *exit*]

Gonzalo Right now I'd give a hundred miles of sea for an acre of barren ground—long heath, dry brush—anything! The will of God be done! But I'd rather die a dry death!

[**Boatswain** *and* **Gonzalo** *exit*]

Act I

Scene II

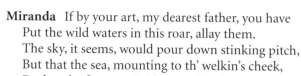

The Island. Before Prospero's Cell. Enter **Prospero** *and* **Miranda**

Miranda If by your art, my dearest father, you have
     Put the wild waters in this roar, allay them.
     The sky, it seems, would pour down stinking pitch,
     But that the sea, mounting to th' welkin's cheek,
5   Dashes the fire out. O, I have suffered

     With those that I saw suffer! A brave vessel,
     Who had, no doubt, some noble creature in her,
     Dashed all to pieces. O, the cry did knock
     Against my very heart! Poor souls, they perished!
10   Had I been any god of power, I would
     Have sunk the sea within the earth, or ere
     It should the good ship so have swallowed, and
     The fraughting souls within her.

Prospero   Be collected;
15   No more amazement: tell your piteous heart
     There's no harm done.

Miranda   O, woe the day!

Prospero   No harm.
     I have done nothing but in care of thee,
20   Of thee, my dear one; thee, my daughter, who
     Art ignorant of what thou art; nought knowing
     Of whence I am, nor that I am more better
     Than Prospero, master of a full poor cell,
     And thy no greater father.

The island. In front of Prospero's cave. **Prospero** *and* **Miranda** *enter.*

Miranda   Dearest father, if you've put the wild waters into a roar by your magic art, then make them still. The sky seems as if it would pour down stinking, fiery pitch, but the sea mounts up to the sky's face to dash out the fire. Oh, I have suffered with those that I saw suffer! A brave ship, which, no doubt, had some noble people aboard, dashed all to pieces. Oh, their cries knocked against my very heart! Poor souls, they perished! Had I been a god of power, I would have sunk the sea within the earth before I'd let it swallow up the good ship and the cargo of souls aboard.

Prospero   Collect yourself. Don't be frightened. Tell your pitying heart that no harm's been done.

Miranda   Oh, how sad the day!

Prospero   No harm's been done. I've done nothing except to take care of you. Of you, my dear one, you, my daughter, who know nothing of who you are, know nothing of where I came from, nor that I am of a higher rank than Prospero, master of a very poor cave, and your humble father.

25 **Miranda**   More to know
    Did never meddle with my thoughts.

    Prospero   'Tis time
    I should inform thee farther. Lend thy hand,
    And pluck my magic garment from me. So:

                          [Lays down his mantle]

30   Lie there, my Art. Wipe thou thine eyes; have comfort.
    The direful spectacle of the wrack, which touched
    The very virtue of compassion in thee,
    I have with such provision in mine Art
    So safely ordered, that there is no soul –
35   No, not so much perdition as an hair –
    Betid to any creature in the vessel
    Which thou heard'st cry, which thou saw'st sink. Sit down;
    For thou must now know farther.

    Miranda   You have often
40   Begun to tell me what I am, but stopped,
    And left me to a bootless inquisition,
    Concluding, 'Stay; not yet'.

    Prospero   The hour's now come;
    The very minute bids thee ope thine ear;
45   Obey, and be attentive. Canst thou remember
    A time before we came unto this cell?
    I do not think thou canst, for then thou wast not
    Out three years old.

    Miranda   Certainly, sir, I can.

50 **Prospero** By what? By any other house or person?
    Of anything the image tell me, that
    Hath kept with thy remembrance.

    Miranda   'Tis far off,
    And rather like a dream than an assurance
55   That my remembrance warrants. Had I not
    Four or five women once that tended me?

Miranda It never entered my thoughts that there was more to know.

Prospero It's time that I should tell you more. Lend me your hand and take my magic cloak from me. So: [*He lays down his cloak*] Lie there, my cloak of magic. Wipe your eyes. Be comforted. Through my magic, I've made safely sure that no evil comes to any soul aboard the ship in that terrible spectacle of the shipwreck, which touched the depths of compassion in you. Not so much as one hair of their heads has come to any harm, even though you've heard their cries and saw the vessel sink. Sit down. You must now know more.

Miranda You've often begun to tell me who I am, but stopped and left me with unanswered questions, saying, "Wait. Not yet."

Prospero The hour's now come. The very minute tells you to open your ear. Obey, and listen carefully. Can you remember a time before we came to this place? I don't think you can, for you weren't yet three years old then.

Miranda Certainly, sir, I can.

Prospero What? Another house or person? Tell me anything that you can remember.

Miranda It seems far off, more like a dream than like a certainty my memory guarantees. Did I once have four or five women who took care of me?

35

Prospero Thou hadst, and more, Miranda. But how is it
    That this lives in thy mind? What seest thou else
    In the dark backward and abysm of time?
60   If thou rememb'rest aught ere thou cam'st here,
    How thou cam'st here thou mayst.

Miranda   But that I do not.

Prospero Twelve year since, Miranda, twelve year since,
    Thy father was the Duke of Milan, and
65   A prince of power.

Miranda   Sir, are not you my father?

Prospero Thy mother was a piece of virtue, and
    She said thou wast my daughter; and thy father
    Was Duke of Milan; and his only heir
70   And princess, no worse issued.

Miranda   O the heavens!
    What foul play had we, that we came from thence?
    Or blessed was't we did?

Prospero   Both, both, my girl;
75   By foul play, as thou say'st, were we heaved thence,
    But blessedly holp hither.

Miranda   O, my heart bleeds
    To think o' th' teen that I have turned you to,
    Which is from my remembrance! Please you, farther.

80 **Prospero** My brother, and thy uncle, called Antonio –
    I pray thee, mark me, that a brother should
    Be so perfidious! – he whom next thyself
    Of all the world I loved, and to him put
    The manage of my state; as at that time
85   Through all the signories it was the first,
    And Prospero the prime duke, being so reputed
    In dignity, and for the liberal Arts
    Without a parallel; those being all my study,

Prospero You had, and more, Miranda. But why does this stay in your mind? What else can you see in the dark and distant past? If you can remember something about the time before you came here, then you may remember how you came here.

Miranda But I don't.

Prospero Twelve years ago, Miranda, twelve years ago, your father was the Duke of Milan, and a prince of power.

Miranda Sir, aren't you my father?

Prospero Your mother was most chaste, and she said you were my daughter. And your father was Duke of Milan. And his only heir was you, a princess no less noble than he.

Miranda Oh heavens! What foul play happened to us that we had to leave? Or was it a blessing that we left?

Prospero Both, both, my girl! We were thrown out by foul play, as you said. But blessed providence helped us to come here.

Miranda Oh, my heart bleeds to think of the sorrow I must have reminded you of, which I can't remember. Please, won't you tell me more.

Prospero My brother—and your uncle—was called Antonio. Mark me well—that a brother should be so treacherous! He whom I loved more than anyone else in the world, next to yourself! I gave the management of my state to him. Of all the city-states at that time, it was the first, and Prospero was the chief duke, since I had a high reputation and was unequaled in my knowledge of the liberal arts. Since all I

The government I cast upon my brother,
90 And to my state grew stranger, being transported
And rapt in secret studies. Thy false uncle –
Dost thou attend me?

Miranda　　　　　　　　Sir, most heedfully.

Prospero　Being once perfected how to grant suits,
95 How to deny them, who t'advance, and who
To trash for over-topping, new created
The creatures that were mine, I say, or changed 'em,
Or else new formed 'em; having both the key
Of officer and office, set all hearts i' th' state
100 To what tune pleased his ear; that now he was
The ivy which had hid my princely trunk,
And sucked my verdure out on't. Thou attend'st not?

Miranda　O, good sir, I do.

Prospero　　　　　　　　　I pray thee, mark me.
105 I, thus neglecting worldly ends, all dedicated
To closeness and the bettering of my mind
With that which, but by being so retired,
O'er-prized all popular rate, in my false brother
Awaked an evil nature; and my trust,
110 Like a good parent, did beget of him
A falsehood in its contrary, as great
As my trust was; which had indeed no limit,
A confidence sans bound. He being thus lorded,
Not only with what my revenue yielded,
115 But what my power might else exact, like one
Who having into truth, by telling of it,
Made such a sinner of his memory,
To credit his own lie, he did believe
He was indeed the duke; out o' th' substitution,
120 And executing th' outward face of royalty,
With all prerogative – hence his ambition growing –
Dost thou hear?

wished to do was study, I gave the power of government to my brother. I became a stranger in my own state, being carried away with my secret studies. Your deceitful uncle. . . . Are you paying attention to me?

Miranda Sir, most carefully.

Prospero Once he had perfected his skill in how to grant requests, how to deny them, who to promote, and who to keep from being too powerful, he took the people who were mine, I say, or replaced them, or won their loyalty. He had both the key of personal power and the key of the office. He turned all the hearts in the state to the tune he wanted to hear. He became like that parasite, ivy, which hid my princely tree and sucked the vitality out of it. Aren't you listening?

Miranda Oh good sir, I am!

Prospero Please, mark my words. I was so dedicated to my seclusion and to my studies that I neglected worldly matters. Being so retired had greater worth than anyone understood. But it awakened an evil nature in my deceitful brother. My trust in him was like a good parent who has an evil child. My trust—which indeed had no limit, which was like a confidence without bounds—brought out of him a deceitfulness that was just as large as that trust. He became like a lord and grew rich, not only from my income, but from what my power enabled him to take from others. He became like a man who having lied so much begins to believe his own lies. He began to believe he was indeed the Duke, since he had substituted for me and carried out my royal duties, with all the privileges of a prince. Therefore, he grew ambitious. . . . Do you hear me?

Miranda   Your tale, sir, would cure deafness.

Prospero To have no screen between this part he played
125   And him he played it for, he needs will be
       Absolute Milan. Me, poor man, my library
       Was dukedom large enough; of temporal royalties
       He thinks me now incapable; confederates,
       So dry he was for sway, wi' th' King of Naples
130   To give him annual tribute, do him homage,
       Subject his coronet to his crown, and bend
       The dukedom, yet unbowed – alas, poor Milan! –
       To most ignoble stooping.

Miranda   O the heavens!

135 **Prospero** Mark his condition, and th' event; then tell me
       If this might be a brother.

Miranda   I should sin
       To think but nobly of my grandmother:
       Good wombs have borne bad sons.

140 **Prospero**   Now the condition.
       This King of Naples, being an enemy
       To me inveterate, hearkens my brother's suit;
       Which was, that he, in lieu o' th' premises
       Of homage and I know not how much tribute,
145   Should presently extirpate me and mine
       Out of the dukedom, and confer fair Milan,
       With all the honours, on my brother: whereon,
       A treacherous army levied, one midnight
       Fated to th' purpose, did Antonio open
150   The gates of Milan; and, i' th' dead of darkness,
       The ministers for th' purpose hurried thence
       Me and thy crying self.

Miranda   Alack, for pity!
       I, not rememb'ring how I cried out then,
155   Will cry it o'er again: it is a hint
       That wrings mine eyes to't.

Miranda Your tale, sir, would cure deafness.

Prospero To have no difference between acting the part and *being* the person he was acting, he wanted to be the actual Duke of Milan. Me, poor man, my library was a large enough dukedom. He now thought that I was incapable of handling practical administrative affairs. He was so thirsty for power that he allied himself with the King of Naples. He agreed to give the King an annual payment, to give him his loyalty, and to make himself a subject of the King of Naples. Alas, poor Milan! He agreed to make the dukedom, which had been previously independent, subject to humiliating subservience.

Miranda Oh, heavens!

Prospero Look at his agreement and its outcome, then tell me if this is a brother.

Miranda I'd be wrong to think anything but good of my grandmother: Good women have given birth to bad sons.

Prospero Now the agreement. This King of Naples, being a longtime enemy to me, listens to my brother's suggestion. The suggestion was this: In return for pledged loyalty and I don't know how much payment in tribute, the King would immediately remove me and my family out of the dukedom and confer the title of Duke of Milan on my brother, with all its honors. Then a treacherous army was raised, and one fateful midnight Antonio opened the gates of Milan. In the dead of darkness, his agents hurried us through them—me and your crying self.

Miranda Alas, how pitiful! I don't remember how I cried then, but I'll cry over it again. It's an occasion that brings tears to my eyes.

Prospero   Hear a little further,
And then I'll bring thee to the present business
Which now's upon us; without the which, this story
160   Were most impertinent.

Miranda   Wherefore did they not
That hour destroy us?

Prospero   Well demanded, wench:
My tale provokes that question. Dear, they durst not,
165   So dear the love my people bore me; nor set
A mark so bloody on the business; but
With colours fairer painted their foul ends.
In few, they hurried us aboard a bark,
Bore us some leagues to sea; where they prepared
170   A rotten carcass of a butt, not rigged,
Nor tackle, sail, nor mast; the very rats
Instinctively have quit it: there they hoist us,
To cry to th' sea that roared to us; to sigh
To th' winds, whose pity, sighing back again,
175   Did us but loving wrong.

Miranda   Alack, what trouble
Was I then to you!

Prospero   O, a cherubim
Thou wast that did preserve me. Thou didst smile,
180   Infused with a fortitude from heaven,
When I have decked the sea with drops full salt,
Under my burthen groaned; which raised in me
An undergoing stomach, to bear up
Against what should ensue.

185 **Miranda**   How came we ashore?

Prospero By Providence divine.
Some food we had, and some fresh water, that
A noble Neapolitan, Gonzalo,
Out of his charity, who being then appointed

42

Prospero Hear a little more, and then I'll tell you what is happening now, without which this story would be pointless.

Miranda Why didn't they destroy us then?

Prospero Well asked, girl. My tale brings up that question. Dear, they dared not, because my people loved me dearly. Not wanting to make this business bloody, they tried to accomplish their ends with little violence. In short, they hurried us aboard a boat and carried us some distance out to sea. There they prepared a rotten carcass of a tub, with no rigging or tackle, no sails or mast. Even the rats instinctively deserted it. They hoisted us aboard it, to cry to the sea that roared to us and to sigh to the winds—which sighed back again in pity, making us feel worse.

Miranda Alas, what a trouble I was to you then!

Prospero Oh, you were an angel who saved me. You smiled, filled with strength from heaven, when I cried salt tears over the sea, groaning under my burdens. Your smile raised in me the courage to endure what was to come.

Miranda How did we come ashore?

Prospero With God's help! We had some food and some fresh water that were given to us by Gonzalo, a noble man of Naples who was put in charge of the operation. He also gave

190 Master of this design, did give us, with
     Rich garments, linens, stuffs and necessaries,
     Which since have steaded much; so, of his gentleness,
     Knowing I loved my books, he furnished me
     From mine own library with volumes that
195 I prize above my dukedom.

Miranda   Would I might
     But ever see that man!

Prospero   Now I arise;
     Sit still, and hear the last of our sea-sorrow.
200 Here in this island we arrived; and here
     Have I, thy schoolmaster, made thee more profit
     Than other princess' can, that have more time
     For vainer hours, and tutors not so careful.

Miranda Heavens thank you for't! And now, I pray you, sir,
205 For still 'tis beating in my mind, your reason
     For raising this sea-storm?

Prospero   Know thus far forth.
     By accident most strange, bountiful Fortune,
     Now my dear lady, hath mine enemies
210 Brought to this shore; and by my prescience
     I find my zenith doth depend upon
     A most auspicious star, whose influence
     If now I court not, but omit, my fortunes
     Will ever after droop. Here cease more questions.
215 Thou art inclined to sleep; 'tis a good dulness,
     And give it way: I know thou canst not choose.

                              [**Miranda** *sleeps*]

     Come away, servant, come. I am ready now.
     Approach, my Ariel, come.

     [*Enter* **Ariel**]

us rich clothing, linens, and other necessities that have been
so useful to us. Out of his gentlemanly character, knowing
that I loved my books, he gave me volumes from my library
that I prize above my dukedom.

Miranda I would like to see that man some day!

Prospero [*rising*] Now I arise. You sit still and hear the last of
our sorrows at sea. We arrived here on this island. And here,
as your schoolmaster, I have given you a more profitable
education than other princesses have, for they have more
time for silly pursuits and their tutors are not as careful.

Miranda And the heavens thank you for it. And now, please
sir—for it is still troubling my mind—what is your reason for
raising this sea storm?

Prospero You may know this much for now. By a strange
accident, bountiful Lady Fortune—she who is now favorable
to me—has brought my enemies to this shore. By my psychic
abilities I see that my height of fortune depends on a star of
good omen. I must take advantage of its power now or
forever after have bad luck. Now, stop asking questions. You
feel like sleeping. It's a pleasant sleepiness. Give it its way. I
know you can't choose otherwise.

[**Miranda** *sleeps*]

Come here, servant, come. I am ready now. Approach, my
Ariel. Come.

[**Ariel** *enters*]

Ariel   All hail, great master! Grave sir, hail! I come
220   To answer thy best pleasure; be 't to fly,
         To swim, to dive into the fire, to ride
         On the curled clouds, to thy strong bidding task
         Ariel and all his quality.

Prospero   Hast thou, spirit,
225   Performed to point the tempest that I bade thee?

Ariel   To every article.
         I boarded the king's ship; now on the beak,
         Now in the waist, the deck, in every cabin,
         I flamed amazement; sometime I'd divide,
230   And burn in many places; on the topmast,
         The yards and bowsprit, would I flame distinctly,
         Then meet and join. Jove's lightnings, the precursors
         O' th' dreadful thunder-claps, more momentary
         And sight-outrunning were not; the fire and cracks
235   Of sulphurous roaring the most mighty Neptune
         Seem to besiege, and make his bold waves tremble,
         Yea, his dread trident shake.

Prospero   My brave spirit!
         Who was so firm, so constant, that this coil
240   Would not infect his reason?

Ariel   Not a soul
         But felt a fever of the mad, and played
         Some tricks of desperation. All but mariners
         Plunged in the foaming brine, and quit the vessel,
245   Then all afire with me. The King's son, Ferdinand,
         With hair up-staring – then like reeds, not hair –
         Was the first man that leaped; cried, 'Hell is empty,
         And all the devils are here!'

Prospero   Why, that's my spirit!
250   But was not this nigh shore?

Ariel   Close by, my master.

Ariel All hail, great master! Revered sir, hail! I come to answer your pleasure. Whether you command us to fly, to swim, to dive into the fire, or to ride on the curled clouds, Ariel and all his fellow spirits will do the task that you bid.

Prospero Spirit, have you carried out in detail the tempest that I ordered?

Ariel To the smallest detail! I boarded the king's ship. On the prow, amidships, on the deck, and in every cabin—I appeared as flames, striking terror. Sometimes I'd split apart and burn in many places. On the topmast, the yardarms, and bowsprit, I'd appear as distinct flames, then meet and join. The god Jove's lightning bolts, coming before the dreadful thunderclaps, were no more brilliantly flashing or more numerous. The fire and the cracking, thundering roar seemed to besiege the god of the sea, most mighty Neptune. They made his bold waves tremble and his dreadful trident shake.

Prospero My brave spirit! Who was so firm, so steady, that this uproar did not affect him?

Ariel There wasn't a soul who did not feel a fever of madness and behave desperately. All of them except the sailors plunged into the foaming brine and abandoned the ship, which was then all in flames from my fire. The King's son, Ferdinand, with his hair standing on end—more like reeds than hair—was the first man that leaped, crying, "Hell is empty, and all the devils are here!"

Prospero Why that's my spirit! But wasn't this near the shore?

Ariel Close by, my master.

Prospero But are they, Ariel, safe?

Ariel   Not a hair perished;
On their sustaining garments not a blemish,
255   But fresher than before; and, as thou bad'st me,
In troops I have dispersed them 'bout the isle.
The King's son have I landed by himself;
Whom I left cooling of the air with sighs
In an odd angle of the isle, and sitting,
260   His arms in this sad knot.

Prospero   Of the King's ship,
The mariners, say how thou hast disposed,
And all the rest o' th' fleet.

Ariel   Safely in harbour
265   Is the King's ship; in the deep nook, where once
Thou call'dst me up at midnight to fetch dew
From the still-vexed Bermoothes, there she's hid:
The mariners all under hatches stowed;
Who, with a charm joined to their suffered labour,
270   I have left asleep; and for the rest o' th' fleet,
Which I dispersed, they all have met again,
And are upon the Mediterranean flote,
Bound sadly home for Naples;
Supposing that they saw the King's ship wracked,
275   And his great person perish.

Prospero   Ariel, thy charge
Exactly is performed; but there's more work.
What is the time o' th' day?

Ariel   Past the mid season.

280   **Prospero** At least two glasses. The time 'twixt six and now
Must by us both be spent most preciously.

Ariel Is there more toil? Since thou dost give me pains,
Let me remember thee what thou hast promised,
Which is not yet performed me.

Prospero But are they safe, Ariel?

Ariel Not a hair on their heads was harmed. There isn't a spot on their clothes, which helped them float; their clothes are fresher than before. I spread them about the island in groups, as you told me. I landed the King's son by himself. I left him cooling the air with his sighs in an odd corner of the island, and sitting with his arms folded in a sad knot, like this. [**Ariel** *demonstrates*]

Prospero Tell me what you've done with the King's ship, the sailors, and the rest of the fleet.

Ariel The King's ship is safely in harbor. She's hidden in a deep cove, where once you conjured me up at midnight to fetch dew from the stormy Bermudas. The sailors are all stowed below deck. I've left them asleep, through a magic spell that combines with their exhaustion from their labor. The rest of the fleet, which I had scattered, have all met again and are on the Mediterranean Sea, bound sadly home for Naples. They believed that they saw the King's ship wrecked and saw the King himself perish.

Prospero Ariel, your work has been performed exactly. But there's more work. What time of day is it?

Ariel Past noon.

Prospero At least two hourglasses past. We both must carefully spend the time between now and six o'clock tonight.

Ariel Is there more work? Since you give me so many duties, let me remind you what you have promised and which you've haven't yet done for me.

285 **Prospero**   How now? Moody?
What is't thou canst demand?

Ariel   My liberty.

Prospero Before the time be out? No more!

Ariel   I prithee,
290   Remember I have done thee worthy service;
Told thee no lies, made no mistakings, served
Without or grudge or grumblings: thou did promise
To bate me a full year.

Prospero   Dost thou forget
295   From what a torment I did free thee?

Ariel   No.

Prospero Thou dost, and think'st it much to tread the ooze
Of the salt deep,
To run upon the sharp wind of the north,
300   To do me business in the veins o' th' earth
When it is baked with frost.

Ariel   I do not, sir.

Prospero Thou liest, malignant thing! Hast thou forgot
The foul witch Sycorax, who with age and envy
305   Was grown into a hoop? Hast thou forgot her?

Ariel No, sir.

Prospero   Thou hast. Where was she born? Speak: tell me.

Ariel Sir, in Argier.

Prospero   O, was she so? I must
310   Once in a month recount what thou hast been,
Which thou forget'st. This damned witch Sycorax,
For mischiefs manifold, and sorceries terrible
To enter human hearing, from Argier,
Thou know'st, was banished: for one thing she did
315   They would not take her life. Is not this true?

Prospero What? Moody? What is it that you can demand?

Ariel My liberty.

Prospero Before your time is up? No more of that!

Ariel I ask you, remember that I have done you worthy service. I've told you no lies, made no mistakes, and served without grudge or grumblings. You did promise to free me a full year early.

Prospero Do you forget from what torment I freed you?

Ariel No.

Prospero You do. And now you think it's too much to walk on the mud of the ocean floor, to ride upon the sharp wind of the north, to do my business in the deep underground streams of the earth when it is hard with frost.

Ariel I do not, sir.

Prospero You lie, you wicked thing! Have you forgotten the foul witch Sycorax, who was so bent over with old age and spitefulness? Have you forgotten her?

Ariel No, sir.

Prospero You have. Where was she born? Speak: Tell me!

Ariel Sir, in Algiers.

Prospero Oh, was she? Once a month I must repeat what you have been, which you forget. For untold numbers of evil deeds and for sorceries too terrible for humans to hear, this damned witch, Sycorax, was banished from Algiers, as you know. They would not take her life because of one thing. Isn't this true?

Ariel Ay, sir.

Prospero This blue-eyed hag was hither brought with child,
    And here was left by th' sailors. Thou, my slave,
    As thou report'st thyself, was then her servant;
320   And, for thou wast a spirit too delicate
    To act her earthy and abhorred commands,
    Refusing her grand hests, she did confine thee,
    By help of her more potent ministers,
    And in her most unmitigable rage,
325   Into a cloven pine; within which rift
    Imprisoned thou didst painfully remain
    A dozen years; within which space she died,
    And left thee there; where thou didst vent thy groans
    As fast as mill-wheels strike. Then was this island –
330   Save for the son that she did litter here,
    A freckled whelp hag-born – not honoured with
    A human shape.

Ariel   Yes, Caliban her son.

Prospero Dull thing I say so; he, that Caliban,
335   Whom now I keep in service. Thou best know'st
    What torment I did find thee in; thy groans
    Did make wolves howl, and penetrate the breasts
    Of ever-angry bears: it was a torment
    To lay upon the damned, which Sycorax
340   Could not again undo: it was mine Art,
    When I arrived and heard thee, that made gape
    The pine, and let thee out.

Ariel   I thank thee, master.

Prospero If thou more murmur'st, I will rend an oak,
345   And peg thee in his knotty entrails, till
    Thou hast howled away twelve winters.

Ariel   Pardon, master:
    I will be correspondent to command,
    And do my spriting gently.

Ariel Yes, sir.

Prospero This sunken-eyed hag was brought here pregnant and was left here by the sailors. You—my slave, as you call yourself—were then her servant. And because you were a spirit too delicate to carry out her earthy and horrible commands, you refused to obey her orders. In her most uncontrollable rage and with the help of her powerful agents, she locked you into a split pine tree. You remained painfully imprisoned there for a dozen years. During that time she died and left you there. And you groaned as fast as mill-wheels strike the water. At the time, except for the son that she gave birth to here—a freckled, hag-born whelp—this island had no human beings.

Ariel Yes, Caliban, her son.

Prospero You stupid thing, that's what I'm saying. He, that Caliban, whom I now keep as a servant. You know best in what torment I found you. Your groans made wolves howl and touched the hearts of the ever-angry bears. It was a torment fit for the damned, which Sycorax could not undo. It was my artful magic, when I arrived and heard you, that made the pine open wide and let you out.

Ariel I thank you, master.

Prospero If you complain any more, I'll split an oak and nail you into its knotty insides until you've howled away twelve winters.

Ariel Pardon, master. I'll be obedient to your commands, and perform my duties as a spirit without grudge.

350 **Prospero**   Do so; and after two days
     I will discharge thee.

     Ariel   That's my noble master!
         What shall I do? Say what: what shall I do?

     Prospero Go make thyself like a nymph o' th' sea:
355   But subject to
         No sight but thine and mine; invisible
         To every eyeball else. Go take this shape,
         And hither come in't: Go, hence with diligence.

                                    [*Exit* **Ariel**]

         Awake, dear heart, awake! Thou hast slept well;
360   Awake!

     Miranda The strangeness of your story put
         Heaviness in me.

     Prospero   Shake it off. Come on;
         We'll visit Caliban my slave, who never
365   Yields us kind answer.

     Miranda   'Tis a villain, sir,
         I do not love to look on.

     Prospero   But, as 'tis,
         We cannot miss him; he does make our fire,
370   Fetch in our wood, and serves in offices
         That profit us. What, ho! slave! Caliban!
         Thou earth, thou! Speak!

     Caliban [*Within*]   There's wood enough within.

     Prospero Come forth, I say! There's other business for thee;
375   Come, thou tortoise! When?

         [*Enter* **Ariel** *like a water-nymph*]

Prospero Do so, and after two days I'll release you.

Ariel That's my noble master! What shall I do? Say what! What shall I do?

Prospero Go make yourself like a sea nymph, but appear to no one's sight but yours and mine. Be invisible to every other eyeball. Go take this shape and come back in it. Go on, with patience.

[**Ariel** *exits*]

[*To* **Miranda**] Awake, dear heart, awake! You have slept well. Awake!

Miranda The strangeness of your story caused a heavy drowsiness in me.

Prospero Shake it off. Come on. We'll visit my slave Caliban, who never gives us a kind answer.

Miranda He's a villain, sir. I don't like to look at him.

Prospero But as it is, we can't get along without him. He does make our fire, fetch our wood, and serve us in ways that are useful. What, hey! Slave! Caliban! You lump of dirt, you! Speak!

Caliban [*out of sight*] There's wood enough inside.

Prospero Come out, I said! There are other things for you to do. Come on, you tortoise! Are you coming?

[**Ariel** *enters in the shape of a sea nymph*]

Fine apparition! My quaint Ariel,
Hark in thine ear.

Ariel   My lord, it shall be done.

[*Exit*]

Prospero Thou poisonous slave, got by the devil himself
380   Upon thy wicked dam, come forth!

[*Enter* **Caliban**]

Caliban   As wicked dew as e'er my mother brushed
With raven's feather from unwholesome fen
Drop on you both! A south-west blow on ye
And blister you all o'er!

385 **Prospero** For this, be sure, to-night thou shalt have cramps,
Side-stitches that shall pen thy breath up; urchins
Shall, for that vast of night that they may work,
All exercise on thee; thou shalt be pinched
As thick as honeycomb, each pinch more stinging
390   Than bees that made 'em.

Caliban   I must eat my dinner.
This island's mine, by Sycorax my mother,
Which thou takest from me. When thou cam'st first,
Thou strok'st me, and made much of me; wouldst give me
395   Water with berries in 't; and teach me how
To name the bigger light, and how the less,
That burn by day and night: and then I loved thee,
And showed thee all the qualities o' th' isle,
The fresh springs, brine-pits, barren place and fertile:
400   Cursed be I that did so! All the charms
Of Sycorax, toads, beetles, bats, light on you!
For I am all the subjects that you have,
Which first was mine own King; and here you sty me
In this hard rock, whiles you do keep from me
405   The rest o' th' island.

A fine appearance! My clever Ariel! Let me have a word in your ear. [*He whispers to* **Ariel**]

Ariel My lord, it shall be done.

[**Ariel** *exits*]

Prospero You poisonous slave, fathered by the devil himself with your wicked mother—come here!

[**Caliban** *enters*]

Caliban May a harmful dew drop on you both—as wicked as any dew that my mother brushed with a raven's feather from a polluted swamp! May the pestilent southwest wind blow on you and blister you all over!

Prospero For saying this, you can be sure that you'll have cramps tonight, side stitches that leave you unable to breathe. Goblins will work on you for that long stretch of the dark night when they may do their evil. You will be pinched until you look like a honeycomb, with each pinch stinging worse than bee stings.

Caliban I must eat my dinner. This island's mine, because of my mother Sycorax, and you took it from me. When you first came, you stroked me and made much of me. You would give me water with berries in it and teach me the name of the bigger light that burns during the day and the smaller light that burns at night. Then I loved you, and I showed you all the things of this island—the fresh springs, the salt pits, the barren places and the fertile places. Curse the fact that I did so! All the charms of Sycorax—toads, beetles, bats—fall on you! I am the only subject that you have. I, who from the first was my own king. And here you confine me in this sty of a cave, while you keep me from the rest of the island.

Prospero   Thou most lying slave,
Whom stripes may move, not kindness! I have used thee,
Filth as thou art, with human care; and lodged thee
In mine own cell, till thou didst seek to violate
410   The honour of my child.

Caliban   O ho, O ho! would't had been done!
Thou didst prevent me; I had peopled else
This isle with Calibans.

Miranda   Abhorred slave,
415   Which any print of goodness wilt not take,
Being capable of all ill! I pitied thee,
Took pains to make thee speak, taught thee each hour
One thing or other: when thou didst not, savage,
Know thine own meaning, but wouldst gabble like
420   A thing most brutish, I endowed thy purposes
With words that made them known. But thy vile race,
Though thou didst learn, had that in't which good natures
Could not abide to be with; therefore wast thou
Deservedly confined into this rock,
425   Who hadst deserved more than a prison.

Caliban   You taught me language; and my profit on't
Is, I know how to curse. The red plague rid you
For learning me your language!

Prospero   Hag-seed, hence!
430   Fetch us in fuel; and be quick, thou'rt best,
To answer other business. Shrug'st thou, malice?
If thou neglect'st, or dost unwillingly
What I command, I'll rack thee with old cramps,
Fill all thy bones with aches, make thee roar,
435   That beasts shall tremble at thy din.

Caliban   No, pray thee.
[*Aside*] I must obey: his Art is of such power,
It would control my dam's god, Setebos,
And make a vassal of him.

Prospero You lying slave, only whipping can make you move, not kindness. Filth as you are, I've treated you with human care and I allowed you to sleep in my own cave, until you tried to rape my daughter.

Caliban Oh ho! Oh ho! I wish I had done it! You prevented me, or else I would have peopled this island with Calibans.

Miranda You horrible slave! Goodness can't leave its print on you. You are capable of all kinds of evil. I pitied you, took pains to teach you to speak. Every hour of the day I taught you one thing or another. When you, savage, didn't know how to make meaningful sounds, but would gabble like a brute, I taught you how to speak and to make your thoughts known. But, even though you did learn, your vile nature had something in it that people of good natures could not stand to be around. Therefore you were deservedly confined in this cave, even though you deserved more punishment than a prison.

Caliban You taught me language. And all I've gained from it is that I know how to curse. May the plague of red sores destroy you for teaching me your language!

Prospero You son of a hag, get out of here! Get us fuel! And you'd better be quick about your business! Do you shrug, you malicious thing? If you neglect your work or do it unwillingly, I'll rack you with cramps like old folks have, fill all your bones with aches, and make you roar so that the beasts will tremble at the noise.

Caliban No, please. [*To himself*] I have to obey. His magic is so powerful it could control my mother's god, Setebos, and make a servant of him.

440 **Prospero**   So, slave; hence!

[*Exit* **Caliban**]

[*Enter* **Ariel,** *invisible, playing and singing;* **Ferdinand**
following]

Ariel   *Come unto these yellow sands,*
                   And then take hands:
                   Curtsied when you have and kissed
                   The wild waves whist:
445   *Foot it featly here and there,*
                   And sweet sprites bear
                   The burthen. Hark, hark.

[*Burthen dispersedly*] *Bow-wow.*

Ariel   *The watch dogs bark:*

450 [*Burthen dispersedly*] *Bow-wow.*

Ariel   *Hark, hark! I hear*
                   The strain of strutting chanticleer

Cry – [*Burthen dispersedly*] *Cock a diddle dow.*

Ferdinand Where should this music be? i' th' air or th' earth?
455   It sounds no more: and, sure, it waits upon
      Some god o' th' island. Sitting on a bank,
      Weeping again the King my father's wrack,
      This music crept by me upon the waters,
      Allaying both their fury and my passion
460   With its sweet air: thence I have followed it,
      Or it hath drawn me rather. But 'tis gone.
      No, it begins again.

Ariel   *Full fathom five thy father lies;*
                   Of his bones are coral made;
465   *Those are pearls that were his eyes:*

Prospero   So, slave, go!

[**Caliban** *exits*]

[**Ariel** *enters, invisible, playing and singing.* **Ferdinand** *follows him*]

Ariel   *Come unto these yellow sands,*
                 And then take hands:
               Curtsy when you have and kiss
                 The wild waves hushed.
               Dance nimbly here and there,
                 And sweet spirits sing
               The chorus. Hark, Hark.

Chorus   [*sung offstage*] *Bow-wow!*

Ariel   *The watchdogs bark.*

Chorus   *Bow-wow!*

Ariel   *Hark, hark! I hear*
               The crow of the strutting cock
               Cry:

Chorus   *Cock-a-doodle-do!*

Ferdinand   Where is this music from? The air or the earth? I don't hear it anymore. Surely, it's meant for some god of this island. As I was sitting on the bank, weeping again over the King my father's shipwreck, this music crept up on me over the waters. Its sweet sound quieted both the storm's fury and my sorrow. Therefore I've followed it. Or rather, it has pulled me. But it is gone. . . . No, it begins again!

Ariel   *Five fathoms deep your father lies;*
                 Of his bones are corals made.
               Those are pearls that were his eyes.

> *Nothing of him that doth fade,*
> *But doth suffer a sea-change*
> *Into something rich and strange.*
> *Sea-nymphs hourly ring his knell.*

470 [*Burthen*] *Ding-dong.*

Ariel *Hark! now I hear them – Ding-dong, bell.*

Ferdinand The ditty does remember my drowned father.
  This is no mortal business, nor no sound
  That the earth owes: I hear it now above me.

475 **Prospero** The fringed curtains of thine eye advance,
  And say what thou seest yond.

Miranda   What is't? A spirit?
  Lord, how it looks about! Believe me, sir,
  It carries a brave form. But 'tis a spirit.

480 **Prospero** No, wench; it eats and sleeps and hath such senses
  As we have, such. This gallant which thou seest
  Was in the wrack; and, but he's something stained
  With grief – that's beauty's canker – thou mightst call him
  A goodly person; he hath lost his fellows,
485 And strays about to find 'em.

Miranda   I might call him
  A thing divine; for nothing natural
  I ever saw so noble.

Prospero [*Aside*]   It goes on, I see,
490 As my soul prompts it. Spirit, fine spirit! I'll free thee
  Within two days for this.

Ferdinand   Most sure the goddess
  On whom these airs attend! Vouchsafe my prayer
  May know if you remain upon this island;
495 And that you will some good instruction give
  How I may bear me here: my prime request,
  Which I do last pronounce, is, O you wonder!
  If you be maid or no?

> *Nothing of him will truly fade,*
> *But the sea has caused a change*
> *Into something rich and strange.*
> *Sea nymphs hourly ring his knell—*

Chorus *Ding-dong . . .*

Ariel *Hark! Now I hear them—Ding-dong, bell.*

Ferdinand The song is in memory of my drowned father. This is no mortal thing, nor a sound that belongs to the earth! I hear it now, above me.

Prospero [*to* **Miranda**] Open the fringed curtains of your eyes. Say what you see there.

Miranda [*seeing* **Ferdinand**] What is it? A spirit? Lord, how it looks about! Believe me, sir, it has a splendid form. But it's a spirit.

Prospero No, girl, it eats and sleeps and has the same senses that we have. This young man that you see was in the shipwreck. And, except for being rather marked with grief—which disfigures beauty—you might call him a good-looking person. He has lost his companions and wanders around trying to find them.

Miranda I might call him a divine creature, for I've never seen anything belonging to this earth that's so noble.

Prospero [*to himself*] The charm is working, I see, as I intended. Spirit, fine spirit! I'll free you within two days for this!

Ferdinand Most surely this is the goddess whom this music serves! [*To* **Miranda**] Would you be gracious enough to answer me this: May I know if you live on this island? And will you instruct me as to how I should behave here? And my most important question—which I ask last—is, oh, you wonderful creature! Are you a maiden, and not a goddess?

Miranda　　　　　　　　No wonder, sir;
500　　But certainly a maid.

Ferdinand　　　　　　　My language! Heavens!
I am the best of them that speak this speech,
Were I but where 'tis spoken.

Prospero　　　　　　　　How? the best?
505　　What wert thou, if the King of Naples heard thee?

Ferdinand　A single thing, as I am now, that wonders
To hear thee speak of Naples. He does hear me;
And that he does I weep; myself am Naples,
Who with mine eyes, never since at ebb, beheld
510　　The King my father wracked.

Miranda　　　　　　　　　Alack, for mercy!

Ferdinand　Yes, faith, and all his lords; the Duke of Milan
And his brave son being twain.

Prospero　[*Aside*]　　　　　The Duke of Milan
515　　And his more braver daughter could control thee,
If now 'twere fit to do't. At the first sight
They have changed eyes. Delicate Ariel,
I'll set thee free for this. [*To* **Ferdinand**] A word, good sir;
I fear you have done yourself some wrong; a word.

520　**Miranda**　Why speaks my father so ungently? This
Is the third man that e'er I saw; the first
That e'er I sighed for: pity move my father
To be inclined my way!

Ferdinand　　　　　　　O, if a virgin,
525　　And your affection not gone forth, I'll make you
The Queen of Naples.

Prospero　　　　　　　Soft, sir! one word more.
[*Aside*] They are both in either's powers: but this swift
　　business
530　　I must uneasy make, lest too light winning

Miranda Not "wonderful," sir, but certainly a maiden.

Ferdinand My own language! Good heavens! I am the highest-ranking person of those who speak this language—if I were where it is spoken.

Prospero What? The highest? What would you be if the King of Naples heard you say that?

Ferdinand A thing alone, as I am now, who is amazed to hear you speak of the King of Naples. He *does* hear me. And I weep because he does. I myself am King of Naples, for I saw my father the King shipwrecked with my own eyes. Since then, they have never been dry.

Miranda Alas, for mercy's sake!

Ferdinand Yes, truly, and all his lords: the Duke of Milan and his brave son being two of them.

Prospero [*to himself*] The Duke of Milan and his even braver daughter could prove the contrary, if now were the right time to do it. [*Referring to* **Ferdinand** *and* **Miranda**] They have exchanged lovers' glances at first sight. Delicate Ariel, I'll set you free for this. [*To* **Ferdinand**] A word, good sir. I fear you have said something mistaken. A word . . .

Miranda Why does my father speak so unkindly? This is the third man I've ever seen, and the first that I've ever sighed for. May pity move my father to consider me.

Ferdinand Oh, if you're a virgin, and you have not given your affection to someone else, I'll make you Queen of Naples.

Prospero Wait, sir! One more word with you . . . [*To himself*] They are both in each other's power. But I must make things difficult for this fast-moving affair, or else winning the prize

Make the prize light. [*To* **Ferdinand**] One word more:
   I charge thee
That thou attend me: thou dost here usurp
The name thou ow'st not; and hast put thyself
535   Upon this island as a spy, to win it
From me, the lord on't.

Ferdinand   No, as I am a man.

Miranda There's nothing ill can dwell in such a temple:
   If the ill spirit have so fair a house,
540   Good things will strive to dwell with't.

Prospero   Follow me.
   Speak not you for him: he's a traitor. Come;
   I'll manacle thy neck and feet together:
   Sea-water shalt thou drink; thy food shall be
545   The fresh-brook mussels, withered roots, and husks
   Wherein the acorn cradled. Follow.

Ferdinand   No;
   I will resist such entertainment till
   Mine enemy has more power.

[*He draws, and is charmed from moving*]

550 **Miranda**   O dear father,
   Make not too rash a trial of him, for
   He's gentle, and not fearful.

Prospero   What! I say,
   My foot my tutor? Put thy sword up, traitor;
555   Who makest a show, but darest not strike, thy conscience
   Is so possessed with guilt: come from thy ward;
   For I can here disarm thee with this stick
   And make thy weapon drop.

Miranda   Beseech you, father.

560 **Prospero** Hence! Hang not on my garments.

easily may make it seem of little value. [*To* **Ferdinand**] One more word: Pay attention. You are using a name that doesn't belong to you. You've come to this island as a spy, to take it from me, the island's lord!

Ferdinand No, as I am a man!

Miranda Nothing evil can live in such a temple! If an evil spirit had such a fair house, good would fight to live in it.

Prospero Follow me. Don't speak to me in his defense. He's a traitor. [*To* **Ferdinand**] Come. I'll chain your neck and feet together. You'll drink sea water. Your food will be freshwater mussels, withered roots, and acorn husks. Follow.

Ferdinand No. I'll fight that kind of treatment until my enemy has more power than I.

[*He draws his sword, but a charm keeps him from moving*]

Miranda Oh, dear father! Don't make things too hard for him. He's a gentleman, and no one to fear.

Prospero What! I say, should I be lectured by my underling? Put your sword up, traitor. You make a show, but you don't dare strike, because your conscience is so full of guilt. Drop your defense! I can disarm you with this wand and make you drop your weapon.

Miranda I beg you, father . . .

Prospero Get away! Don't hang onto my clothes.

Miranda   Sir, have pity;
  I'll be his surety.

Prospero   Silence! One word more
  Shall make me chide thee, if not hate thee. What!
565 And advocate for an impostor! Hush!
  Thou think'st there is no more such shapes as he,
  Having seen but him and Caliban: foolish wench!
  To th' most of men this is a Caliban,
  And they to him are angels.

570 **Miranda**   My affections
  Are then most humble; I have no ambition
  To see a goodlier man.

Prospero   Come on; obey;
  Thy nerves are in their infancy again,
575 And have no vigour in them.

Ferdinand   So they are:
  My spirits, as in a dream, are all bound up.
  My father's loss, the weakness which I feel,
  The wrack of all my friends, nor this man's threats,
580 To whom I am subdued, are but light to me,
  Might I but through my prison once a day
  Behold this maid: all corners else o' th' earth
  Let liberty make use of; space enough
  Have I in such a prison.

585 **Prospero** [*Aside*]   It works.
  [*To* **Ferdinand**] Come on.
  [*To* **Ariel**] Thou hast done well, fine Ariel! Follow me;
  Hark what thou else shalt do me.

Miranda   Be of comfort;
590 My father's of a better nature, sir,
  Than he appears by speech: this is unwonted
  Which now came from him.

Miranda Sir, have pity! I'll guarantee him!

Prospero Silence! One more word will make me scold you, if not hate you! What! Stand up for this impostor? Hush! You think that there are no other men who are so wonderful, having seen just him and Caliban. Foolish girl! Compared to most men, *he* is a Caliban. Compared to him, they are angels.

Miranda My preferences, then, are humble. I have no aim to see a better-looking man.

Prospero [*to* **Ferdinand**] Come along; do as I say. Your muscles are like an infant's again and have no strength in them.

Ferdinand So they are. My vitality is all bound up, like in a dream. The loss of my father, the weakness that I feel, the shipwreck of all my friends, even the threats of this man who has me in chains—all these are small things to me, if I might see this maiden once a day from my prison. All the rest of the world can be free. This prison is space enough.

Prospero [*to himself*] The spell is working! [*To* **Ferdinand**] Come on. [*To* **Ariel**] You have done well, fine Ariel! Follow me. Listen to what else you shall do for me.

Miranda Be comforted. My father's a kinder man than his words make him seem. What he said just now isn't like him.

Prospero   Thou shalt be as free
    As mountain winds: but then exactly do
595   All points of my command.

Ariel   To th' syllable.

Prospero Come, follow. Speak not for him.

[Exeunt]

Prospero [*to* **Ariel**] You shall be as free as the mountain winds, if you carry out exactly every detail that I command.

Ariel To the last syllable.

Prospero [*to* **Ferdinand**] Come, follow me. [*To* **Miranda**] Don't speak in his defense!

[*They exit*]

Comprehension Check What You Know

1. What is the setting of this play?

2. What events have brought Ferdinand to this place?

3. Why are Prospero and Miranda in this place? What special powers does Prospero possess?

4. Describe Caliban. How is he different from the other characters?

5. What tasks does Ariel perform for Prospero?

6. Describe Miranda's reaction when she first sees Ferdinand.

7. At the end of this act, what is your opinion of Prospero? Is he kind or unkind? Is he powerful or weak?

8. What do you know about Miranda? Is she a worldly person? Or has she had limited experiences?

Activities & Role-Playing Classes or Informal Groups

With a Simple Wave Study the lines of Prospero and Ariel in Scene 2. Role-play their parts. Be sure to include any of Prospero's movements with his hands or with props. Also, imagine how he might sound when he speaks to Ariel. Would he use a soft voice or a loud exclamatory tone? For Ariel, imagine the movements and physical expressions. Is Ariel strong or weak in physical nature? To extend the activity, invite other readers to take the parts of Miranda and Ferdinand for particular scenes.

Next Stop, Utopia Research literature and encyclopedias for definitions of *utopia*. Based on your findings, make a list of the characteristics of utopia. If time allows, create a sketch showing what utopia looks like based on your findings or what you imagine utopia to be.

Jacqueline Kim as Miranda, Ted van Griethuysen as Prospero, and Raphael Nash as Caliban in The Shakespeare Theater's 1989 production of *The Tempest* directed by Richard E. T. White. Photo by Joan Marcus.

Discussion **Classes or Informal Groups**

1. In Scene 2, discuss the exchange between Prospero and Caliban. How do these two characters treat each other?

2. Refer to the list of characters and note their home countries. What challenges do you think the characters will face in this new land? What is unfamiliar to them?

3. Prospero explains some of his past in Scene 2. How does he feel about his past?

4. What is Ariel's true goal? What is Prospero's plan for Ariel? Do they disagree? Why or why not?

5. What is the difference between acting of one's own free will and being controlled by outside forces? Discuss events in history that are examples of people fighting to exercise their free will.

Suggestions for Writing **Improve Your Skills**

1. Based on details in Act 1, write a two-sentence description of each character. List clothing, height, and other physical features.

2. Refer to Caliban's speech in Scene 2 (lines 391–405). What do you think he means by "Which first was mine own King" (line 403)? Write a paragraph explaining what you think Caliban means by this phrase. Use other details from this speech to support your explanation.

3. Find examples of free will and outside forces in Act 1. Which characters or events affect the behavior of other characters? Write an analysis of a character of your choosing. Explain whether or not the character is free or affected by outside forces.

All the World's a Stage Introduction

Stranded. Left high and dry. For some of the shipwrecked castaways, Prospero's island feels like ground zero. After all, several of the characters have just attended a royal wedding. They were sailing back to lives of power and wealth at home. Then, it seemed, disaster struck.

In *The Tempest,* whole worlds seem to be at some characters' fingertips. Then they turn out to be out of reach. Alonso has just married his daughter to the King of Tunis, in northern Africa. He has created strong partnerships overseas and in Italy. He had high hopes for Ferdinand, his dear son. Now, he sits on a deserted beach, surrounded by useless advisors. His daughter is far, far away. And he thinks that Ferdinand is drowned.

What's in a Name? Characters

Prospero has used his magic to strand Alonso and Antonio on the island and in his power. This allows Shakespeare to create some interesting parallels and partnerships between characters. For example, Prospero's revenge puts Alonso in a similar situation to the one Prospero had faced—Alonso has gone from high and mighty status to isolation and loss. Prospero and Alonso are also linked because each has a child they care for dearly. And those children are falling in love.

In Act 2, we meet Prospero's scheming brother, Antonio, and his ally, Sebastian, Alonso's brother. This pair is up to no good. Meanwhile, two more rascals, named Trinculo and Stephano, are making some plans of their own. For these two tipsy servants, the island offers a way to become big shots.

COME WHAT MAY Things to Watch For

Where is Prospero's island? In *The Tempest,* references to journeys off the coasts of Italy and Africa make us think Prospero's island is somewhere in the Mediterranean. In some ways, however, Prospero's island is a kind of *utopia.*

A utopia is an ideal place or community. In Greek, *utopia* means "no place." In the 16th and 17th centuries, thinkers like Thomas More and Francis Bacon wrote about utopias on imaginary lands. They envisioned new forms of government and society in these imaginary places. In the 20th century, the English writer Aldous Huxley used a phrase from *The Tempest* as the title of his novel, *Brave New World.* In it, he described a utopian society that went terribly wrong.

As you read, look for signs of utopia on Prospero's island. Decide whether you think this little world could fit with your idea of a perfect place.

All Our Yesterdays Historical and Social Context

For travelers in Shakespeare's time, there were no cameras and video recorders to document a trip. People sent letters by ship, kept diaries, drew pictures, and took home souvenirs.

Some of the specimens and drawings showed exotic plants and animals. They also brought human inhabitants of the Americas back with them. Sometimes they hoped to make some money by putting these people on display. The people, plants, and animals of the New World were considered wonderful curiosity items by rich and poor alike. Scam artists saw a chance to fool a public that was greedy for facts and fiction from the strange new lands.

The Play's the Thing Staging

To those of us raised on the movies, staging *The Tempest* might seem like quite a challenge. In several scenes, Ariel carries out Prospero's orders by using magical powers. Portraying lightning speed and "looking" invisible on stage might seem like tall orders. How did Shakespeare's company show that Ariel couldn't be seen?

This "special effect" might have been achieved very simply. In a list of costumes written by a theater producer of Shakespeare's time, one item describes "a robe for to go invisibell." Audiences probably saw that an actor was wearing a particular costume they knew "stood for" the power to be unseen. Then they let their imaginations do the rest!

My Words Fly Up Language

Even Shakespeare experts are not always sure of his meanings. In Act 2, Antonio and Sebastian poke quite a bit of fun at the kindly Gonzalo. They are especially amused by his remarks about the "widow Dido." Shakespeare and his audience probably found this choice of words funny, too—but scholars today aren't exactly sure why.

In Greek legend, Dido was queen of Carthage, a North African city. She is a famous character in the *Aeneid* (c. 30–19 B.C.), an epic poem by the Roman poet Vergil. He tells how the Trojan prince Aeneas fled Troy and founded Rome. On the way, his ship got blown off course to Carthage. There, he and Dido became lovers. After he left her to continue his journey, Dido killed herself.

Dido really *was* a widow when she met Aeneas. She was also a very passionate woman. When Gonzalo calls this jilted queen "widow Dido," it may be his way of being prim and proper. He may be trying to avoid insulting Alonso's daughter, who is also a North African queen. However, there were also plenty of jokes in Shakespeare's time about lustful, "loose" widows. We may never be quite sure about the point of his humor here.

Act II

Scene I

Another part of the Island. Enter **Alonso, Sebastian, Antonio, Gonzalo, Adrian, Francisco,** *and others*

Gonzalo   Beseech you, sir, be merry; you have cause,
So have we all, of joy; for our escape
Is much beyond our loss. Our hint of woe
Is common; every day, some sailor's wife,
5   The masters of some merchant, and the merchant,
Have just our theme of woe; but for the miracle,
I mean our preservation, few in millions
Can speak like us: then wisely, good sir, weigh
Our sorrow with our comfort.

10   **Alonso**   Prithee, peace.

Sebastian   [*Aside to* **Antonio**]   He receives comfort like cold
porridge.

Antonio   [*Aside to* **Sebastian**]   The visitor will not give him
o'er so.

15   **Sebastian**   [*Aside to* **Antonio**]   Look, he's winding up the
watch of his wit; by and by it will strike.

Gonzalo   Sir –

Sebastian   [*Aside to* **Antonio**]   One: tell.

Gonzalo   When every grief is entertained that's offered,
20   Comes to th' entertainer –

Another part of the island. **Alonso, Sebastian, Antonio, Gonzalo, Adrian, Francisco,** *and others enter.*

Gonzalo I beg you, sir, be cheerful. You have cause for joy, as we all have. Our escape far outweighs our loss. Our cause for sadness is common. Every day, some sailor's wife, the masters of some merchant ship, and the merchant who engaged it have the same reason for grief that we have. But as regards the miracle—I mean our preservation—few people in millions can speak as we do now. Then, good sir, carefully weigh our grief against our comfort.

Alonso Please, hold your peace.

Sebastian [*privately to* **Antonio**] He accepts comfort like it's cold porridge.

Antonio [*privately to* **Sebastian**] The "comforter" will not give up easily.

Sebastian [*privately to* **Antonio**] Look, he's winding up the watch of his wit. It will strike soon.

Gonzalo Sir—

Sebastian [*aside to* **Antonio**] One o'clock! Keep time!

Gonzalo When every grief that's possible is entertained, there comes to the entertainer . . .

Sebastian A dollar.

Gonzalo Dolour comes to him, indeed: you have spoken truer than you purposed.

Sebastian You have taken it wiselier than I meant you
25 should.

Gonzalo Therefore, my lord, –

Antonio Fie, what a spendthrift is he of his tongue!

Alonso I prithee, spare.

Gonzalo Well, I have done; but yet, –

30 **Sebastian** He will be talking.

Antonio Which, of he or Adrian, for a good wager, first begins to crow?

Sebastian The old cock.

Antonio The cockerel.

35 **Sebastian** Done. The wager?

Antonio A laughter.

Sebastian A match!

Adrian Though this island seem to be desert –

Antonio Ha, ha, ha!

40 **Sebastian** So: you're paid!

Adrian Uninhabitable, and almost inaccessible –

Sebastian Yet –

Adrian Yet –

Antonio He could not miss't.

45 **Adrian** It must needs be of subtle, tender and delicate temperance.

Sebastian A dollar payment?

Gonzalo Dolor—sorrow—comes to him indeed. You've spoken truer than you meant.

Sebastian And you've taken it more wisely than I meant.

Gonzalo Therefore, my lord—

Antonio Good grief, how his tongue wags!

Alonso Please, spare me.

Gonzalo Well, I'm done. . . . But yet—

Sebastian He just keeps talking!

Antonio Let's make a good bet. Which one, he or Adrian, will be the first to start crowing?

Sebastian The old cock!

Antonio The cockerel!

Sebastian Done! What's the bet?

Antonio A good laugh!

Sebastian A deal!

Adrian Though this island seems to be uninhabited—

Antonio Ha, ha, ha!

Sebastian So, you're paid!

Adrian Uninhabitable, and almost inaccessible—

Sebastian "Yet"—

Adrian —yet—

Antonio He couldn't avoid saying that!

Adrian It must have a mild and gentle climate—a mild temperance.

Antonio Temperance was a delicate wench.

Sebastian Ay, and a subtle; as he most learnedly delivered.

Adrian The air breathes upon us here most sweetly.

50 **Sebastian** As if it had lungs, and rotten ones.

Antonio Or as 'twere perfumed by a fen.

Gonzalo Here is everything advantageous to life.

Antonio True; save means to live.

Sebastian Of that there's none, or little.

55 **Gonzalo** How lush and lusty the grass looks! how green!

Antonio The ground, indeed, is tawny.

Sebastian With an eye of green in 't.

Antonio He misses not much.

Sebastian No; he doth but mistake the truth totally.

60 **Gonzalo** But the rarity of it is – which is indeed almost
beyond credit –

Sebastian As many vouched rarities are.

Gonzalo That our garments, being, as they were, drenched in
the sea, hold, notwithstanding, their freshness and glosses,
65 being rather new-dyed than stained with salt water.

Antonio If but one of his pockets could speak, would it not
say he lies?

Sebastian Ay, or very falsely pocket up his report.

Gonzalo Methinks our garments are now as fresh as when we
70 put them on first in Afric, at the marriage of the King's fair
daughter Claribel to the King of Tunis.

Sebastian 'Twas a sweet marriage, and we prosper well in
our return.

Antonio Temperance—Yes, she was a gentle girl.

Sebastian Yes, and mild, as he most learnedly said.

Adrian There's a sweet breath of air for us —

Sebastian As if it came right out of rotten lungs.

Antonio Or perfumed by a swamp.

Gonzalo Here there's everything that's advantageous to life.

Antonio True. Except the means to live.

Sebastian There's little or none of that!

Gonzalo How lush and rich the grass looks! How green!

Antonio The ground, indeed, is parched yellow!

Sebastian With a spot of green in it.

Antonio He doesn't miss much.

Sebastian No—he just misses the truth entirely!

Gonzalo But the rare thing about it is—and this is indeed almost beyond belief—

Sebastian As many true rarities are.

Gonzalo That our clothes, in spite of having been soaked in the seas, are still fresh and shiny. They look as if they were newly dyed, rather than stained with salt water.

Antonio If just one of his pockets could speak, wouldn't it say he lies?

Sebastian Yes, or conceal the information by pocketing it.

Gonzalo I think our garments are just as fresh as when we first put them on in Africa, at the marriage of the King's fair daughter, Claribel, to the King of Tunis.

Sebastian It was a sweet marriage, and we enjoyed our return trip.

Adrian Tunis was never graced before with such a paragon to
75   their Queen.

Gonzalo Not since widow Dido's time.

Antonio Widow! a pox o' that! How came that widow in?
Widow Dido!

Sebastian What if he had said 'widower Æneas' too? Good
80   Lord, how you take it!

Adrian 'Widow Dido' said you? You make me study of that:
she was of Carthage, not of Tunis.

Gonzalo This Tunis, sir, was Carthage.

Adrian Carthage?

85 **Gonzalo** I assure you, Carthage.

Antonio His word is more than the miraculous harp.

Sebastian He hath raised the wall, and houses too.

Antonio What impossible matter will he make easy next?

Sebastian I think he will carry this island home in his pocket,
90   and give it his son for an apple.

Antonio And, sowing the kernels of it in the sea, bring forth
more islands.

Gonzalo Ay.

Antonio Why, in good time.

95 **Gonzalo** Sir, we were talking that our garments seem now as
fresh as when we were at Tunis at the marriage of your
daughter, who is now Queen.

Antonio And the rarest that e'er came there.

Sebastian Bate, I beseech you, widow Dido.

100 **Antonio** O, widow Dido! Ay, widow Dido.

Adrian   Tunis was never blessed before with such a model of perfection for their queen.

Gonzalo   Not since widow Dido's time.

Antonio   Widow! A plague on that! How did he come up with "widow"? "Widow" Dido!

Sebastian   What if he had also said "widower Aeneas"? Good Lord, how far will you take this!

Adrian   "Widow Dido" you said? You make me think—she was Queen of Carthage, not Tunis.

Gonzalo   This Tunis, sir, was once called Carthage.

Adrian   Carthage?

Gonzalo   Yes, I assure you—Carthage.

Antonio   His word is more powerful than that miraculous harp that created the walls of the city of Thebes.

Sebastian   He has created the wall, and the houses too!

Antonio   What other impossible thing will he make seem easy?

Sebastian   I think he'll carry this island home in his pocket. He'll give it to his son as an apple.

Antonio   And he'll sow the seeds of it in the sea, growing more islands.

Gonzalo   Yes, indeed, it was Carthage.

Antonio   Very clever!

Gonzalo   Sir, we were saying that our clothing seems to be as fresh now as when we were in Tunis at the marriage of your daughter, who is now the queen.

Antonio   And the rarest one who ever went there.

Sebastian   Except, if you please, the widow Dido.

Antonio   Oh, the widow Dido! Yes, the widow Dido!

Gonzalo Is not, sir, my doublet as fresh as the first day I wore
it? I mean, in a sort.

Antonio That sort was well fished for.

Gonzalo When I wore it at your daughter's marriage?

105 **Alonso** You cram these words into mine ears against
The stomach of my sense. Would I had never
Married my daughter there! For, coming thence,
My son is lost, and, in my rate, she too,
Who is so far from Italy removed
110 I ne'er again shall see her. O thou mine heir
Of Naples and of Milan, what strange fish
Hath made his meal on thee?

Francisco   Sir, he may live:
I saw him beat the surges under him,
115 And ride upon their backs; he trod the water,
Whose enmity he flung aside, and breasted
The surge most swoln that met him; his bold head
'Bove the contentious waves he kept, and oared
Himself with his good arms in lusty stroke
120 To th' shore, that o'er his wave-worn basis bowed,
As stooping to relieve him. I not doubt
He came alive to land.

Alonso   No, no, he's gone.

Sebastian Sir, you may thank yourself for this great loss,
125 That would not bless our Europe with your daughter,
But rather loose her to an African;
Where she, at least, is banished from your eye,
Who hath cause to wet the grief on 't.

Alonso   Prithee, peace.

130 **Sebastian** You were kneeled to, and importuned otherwise,
By all of us; and the fair soul herself
Weighed between loathness and obedience, at
Which end o' th' beam should bow. We have lost your son,

Gonzalo Isn't my jacket as fresh as the first day I wore it? I mean, comparatively speaking.

Antonio You fished well to pull out that "comparatively."

Gonzalo When I wore it at your daughter's marriage?

Alonso You cram these words into my ear as if you were stuffing my stomach against my will. I wish I'd never allowed my daughter to be married there. For my son has been lost on our return, and I believe she's lost too! She's so far away from Italy that I'll never see her again. Oh my heir of Naples and Milan! What strange fish has made a meal of you?

Francisco Sir, he may still live. I saw him beat against the waves and ride upon their backs. He didn't sink, but flung aside the waters and rode the swollen surge of waves. He kept his head above the angry waves and used his arms like oars to row him to the shore, which sloped down, as if stooping to rescue him. I have no doubt that he came to land alive.

Alonso No, no. He's gone.

Sebastian Sir, you may thank yourself for this great loss. You wouldn't bless our Europe with your daughter, but rather gave her to an African. She is gone from your eyes, which is cause enough to cry with the grief of it.

Alonso Please, be quiet.

Sebastian All of us kneeled before you and begged you to do otherwise. The fair girl herself went back and forth between despising the marriage and desiring to be obedient, not knowing which to choose. We've lost your son, I fear, forever.

I fear, for ever: Milan and Naples have
135   More widows in them of this business' making
Than we bring men to comfort them:
The fault's your own.

Alonso   So is the dear'st o' th' loss.

Gonzalo My lord Sebastian,
140   The truth you speak doth lack some gentleness,
And time to speak it in: you rub the sore,
When you should bring the plaster.

Sebastian   Very well.

Antonio And most chirurgeonly.

145 **Gonzalo** It is foul weather in us all, good sir,
    When you are cloudy.

Sebastian   Fowl weather?

Antonio   Very foul.

Gonzalo Had I plantation of this isle, my lord, –

150 **Antonio** He'd sow't with nettle-seed.

Sebastian   Or docks, or mallows.

Gonzalo And were the King on 't, what would I do?

Sebastian 'Scape being drunk for want of wine.

Gonzalo I' th' commonwealth I would by contraries
155   Execute all things; for no kind of traffic
Would I admit; no name of magistrate;
Letters should not be known; riches, poverty,
And use of service, none; contract, succession,
Bourn, bound of land, tilth, vineyard, none;
160   No use of metal, corn, or wine, or oil;
No occupation; all men idle, all;
And women too, but innocent and pure;
No sovereignty –

Because of this business, Milan and Naples now have more widows than we bring back men to comfort them. The fault is all yours.

Alonso So is the most painful loss.

Gonzalo My lord Sebastian, you speak truly, but without gentleness and at the wrong time. You irritate the wound when you should be dressing it.

Sebastian Very well.

Antonio And in the manner of a surgeon.

Gonzalo It's foul weather for all of us, good sir, when you're in a bad mood.

Sebastian Fowl weather?

Antonio Very foul.

Gonzalo If I could make a plantation of this island, my lord—

Antonio He'd sow it with nettles.

Sebastian Or weeds and wild plants.

Gonzalo And if I were king of it, what would I do?

Sebastian Escape being drunk because of the lack of wine.

Gonzalo In my state I'd do everything that's the opposite of custom. I wouldn't allow any trade or business. There would be no one you could call "magistrate." Learning would not be known. There would be no riches, no poverty, and no servants. Contracts, hereditary privileges, boundaries or division of land, planting, vineyards—none. No use of metal, corn, or wine, or oil. No occupation. All men would be idle, all. And women, too, but innocent and pure. There'd be no sovereign rule—

Sebastian   Yet he would be king on 't!

165 **Antonio** The latter end of his commonwealth forgets the
      beginning.

Gonzalo All things in common Nature should produce
      Without sweat or endeavour: treason, felony,
      Sword, pike, knife, gun, or need of any engine,
170   Would I not have; but Nature should bring forth,
      Of it own kind, all foison, all abundance,
      To feed my innocent people.

Sebastian No marrying 'mong his subjects?

Antonio None, man; all idle; whores and knaves.

175 **Gonzalo** I would with such perfection govern, sir,
      T' excel the Golden Age.

Sebastian   Save his Majesty!

Antonio Long live Gonzalo!

Gonzalo   And – do you mark me, sir?

180 **Alonso** Prithee, no more: thou dost talk nothing to me.

Gonzalo I do well believe your highness; and did it to minister
      occasion to these gentlemen, who are of such sensible and
      nimble lungs that they always use to laugh at nothing.

Antonio 'Twas you we laughed at.

185 **Gonzalo** Who in this kind of merry fooling am nothing to
      you; so you may continue, and laugh at nothing still.

Antonio What a blow was there given!

Sebastian An it had not fallen flat-long.

Gonzalo You are gentlemen of brave mettle; you would lift
190   the moon out of her sphere, if she would continue in it five
      weeks without changing.

Sebastian Yet he'd be king of it!

Antonio The end of his commonwealth forgets how it began.

Gonzalo Nature will produce everything for the common good without sweat or labor. I'd have no treason, crime, sword, spear, knife, gun; no need for any engine of war. Nature would bring forth all the plenty, all the abundance, to feed my innocent people.

Sebastian No marrying among his subjects?

Antonio None, man. All would be idle: whores and villains.

Gonzalo I would govern with such perfection, sir, that it would be more excellent than the Golden Age.

Sebastian God save his Majesty!

Antonio Long live Gonzalo!

Gonzalo And—do you hear me, sir?

Alonso Please, no more. You're talking nonsense to me.

Gonzalo I believe you're right, your Highness. I did it to give an opportunity to these gentlemen, who have such sensitive and lively lungs that they laugh at nothing.

Antonio It was *you* we laughed at.

Gonzalo And in this kind of silly fooling around I'm nothing compared to you. So you may continue, and keep laughing at nothing.

Antonio What a witty blow was that!

Sebastian If it hadn't fallen flat!

Gonzalo You gentlemen are so brave! You'd lift the moon out of her orbit, if she continued in it five weeks without changing.

[*Enter* **Ariel,** *invisible, playing solemn music*]

Sebastian We would so, and then go a bat-fowling.

Antonio Nay, good my lord, be not angry.

Gonzalo No, I warrant you; I will not adventure my discretion
195   so weakly. Will you laugh me asleep, for I am very heavy?

Antonio Go sleep, and hear us.

[*All sleep except* **Alonso, Sebastian,** *and* **Antonio**]

Alonso What, all so soon asleep! I wish mine eyes
Would, with themselves, shut up my thoughts: I find
They are inclined to do so.

200 **Sebastian**   Please you, sir,
Do not omit the heavy offer of it:
It seldom visits sorrow; when it doth,
It is a comforter.

Antonio   We two, my lord,
205   Will guard your person while you take your rest,
And watch your safety.

Alonso   Thank you. Wondrous heavy.

[**Alonso** *sleeps. Exit* **Ariel**]

Sebastian What a strange drowsiness possesses them!

Antonio It is the quality o' th' climate.

210 **Sebastian**   Why
Doth it not then our eyelids sink? I find not
Myself disposed to sleep.

[**Ariel** *enters, invisible, playing solemn music*]

Sebastian Yes, we would. And then we'd go bird hunting, using the moon for a lantern.

Antonio Good sir, don't be angry.

Gonzalo No, I guarantee I won't. I won't risk my reputation for good judgment by getting angry over such a small thing. Will you laugh me asleep? I'm very tired.

Antonio Go on to sleep, and hear us laugh.

[*Everyone sleeps except* **Alonso, Sebastian,** *and* **Antonio**]

Alonso What, everyone asleep so soon! I wish my eyes would close and shut out my thoughts. I feel they're inclined to do so.

Sebastian Please, sir, don't resist the opportunity for sleep. Sleep seldom comes to those in sorrow. When it does, it's a comfort.

Antonio My lord, the two of us will guard you while you take your rest. We'll watch out for your safety.

Alonso Thank you. I'm surprisingly sleepy.

[**Alonso** *sleeps*]

[**Ariel** *exits*]

Sebastian What a strange drowsiness overcomes them!

Antonio It's this climate.

Sebastian Then why don't our eyelids droop? I don't find myself feeling sleepy.

Antonio   Nor I; my spirits are nimble.
    They fell together all, as by consent;
215   They dropped, as by a thunder-stroke. What might,
    Worthy Sebastian? O, what might? No more –
    And yet methinks I see it in thy face,
    What thou shouldst be; th' occasion speaks thee; and
    My strong imagination sees a crown
220   Dropping upon thy head.

Sebastian   What, art thou waking?

Antonio Do you not hear me speak?

Sebastian   I do; and surely
    It is a sleepy language, and thou speak'st
225   Out of thy sleep. What is it thou didst say?
    This is a strange repose, to be asleep
    With eyes wide open; standing, speaking, moving,
    And yet so fast asleep.

Antonio   Noble Sebastian,
230   Thou let'st thy fortune sleep – die, rather; wink'st
    Whiles thou art waking.

Sebastian   Thou dost snore distinctly;
    There's meaning in thy snores.

Antonio I am more serious than my custom: you
235   Must be so too, if heed me; which to do
    Trebles thee o'er.

Sebastian   Well, I am standing water.

Antonio I'll teach you how to flow.

Sebastian   Do so: to ebb
240   Hereditary sloth instructs me.

Antonio   O,
    If you but knew how you the purpose cherish
    Whiles thus you mock it! How, in stripping it,

Antonio Nor I. My spirits are lively. They all fell asleep together, as if by mutual consent. They dropped off as if struck by a thunderbolt. What if, worthy Sebastian—? Oh, what if—? No more. . . . And yet I think I see it in your face— what you should be. This occasion gives you an opportunity, and my strong imagination sees a crown dropping upon your head.

Sebastian What, are you awake?

Antonio Don't you hear me speak?

Sebastian I do. But surely it's just sleepy babble, and you're talking in your sleep. What is it that you said? This is a strange slumber, to be asleep with your eyes wide open— standing, speaking, moving, and yet so fast asleep.

Antonio Noble Sebastian, you're letting your good fortune sleep—or rather, you're letting it die. Your eyes are closed while you're awake!

Sebastian You do snore distinctly. There's meaning in your snores.

Antonio I'm more serious than I usually am. You must be, too, if you pay attention to me. If you do, it will triple your fortune.

Sebastian Well, I'm like standing water: not moving this way or that.

Antonio I'll teach you how to flow.

Sebastian Do so. Hereditary laziness makes me tend to ebb.

Antonio Oh, if you but knew how you pine for this even while you mock it. How you dress this up, even as you strip it

You more invest it! Ebbing men, indeed,
245 Most often do so near the bottom run
By their own fear or sloth.

Sebastian   Prithee, say on:
The setting of thine eye and cheek proclaim
A matter from thee; and a birth, indeed,
250 Which throes thee much to yield.

Antonio   Thus, sir:
Although this lord of weak remembrance, this,
Who shall be of as little memory
When he is earthed, hath here almost persuaded –
255 For he's a spirit of persuasion, only
Professes to persuade – the King his son's alive,
'Tis as impossible that he's undrowned
As he that sleeps here swims.

Sebastian   I have no hope
260 That he's undrowned.

Antonio   O, out of that 'no hope'
What great hope have you! No hope that way is
Another way so high a hope, that even
Ambition cannot pierce a wink beyond,
265 But doubt discovery there. Will you grant with me
That Ferdinand is drowned?

Sebastian   He's gone.

Antonio   Then tell me
Who's the next heir of Naples?

270 **Sebastian**   Claribel.

Antonio She that is Queen of Tunis; she that dwells
Ten leagues beyond man's life; she that from Naples
Can have no note, unless the sun were post –
The man i' th' moon's too slow – till new-born chins
275 Be rough and razorable; she that from whom

down! Men who "ebb" are indeed kept at the bottom, held back by their own fear or laziness.

Sebastian Please, say more. The look in your eye and on your face tells me that there's something you want to get out. Indeed, the birth of it causes you much labor pain.

Antonio It's this, sir. [*Indicating* **Gonzalo**] This lord, who has a short memory—this lord who will be just as little remembered when he's dead and buried—has almost persuaded the King that his son's alive. It's his function to persuade, and so he attempts it. But it's impossible to believe that the King's son isn't drowned, as impossible as it is for this man here to swim as he sleeps.

Sebastian I have no hope that the King's son is not drowned.

Antonio Oh, what a great hope you have, which comes out of that "no hope"! To have no hope that Ferdinand isn't drowned is, in another way, to have such a high hope that even ambition can't glimpse beyond it, it's so unbelievable. Will you agree that Ferdinand is drowned?

Sebastian He's gone.

Antonio Then tell me, who's the next heir of Naples?

Sebastian Claribel.

Antonio She who is queen of Tunis. She who lives more than a lifetime's journey away. She who can't get news from Naples any faster than it takes a baby to become a young man (unless the sun acted as messenger, for the Man in the Moon is too slow). She from whom we were sailing when we were

We all were sea-swallowed, though some cast again,
And that by destiny, to perform an act
Whereof what's past is prologue; what to come,
Is yours and my discharge.

280 **Sebastian**   What stuff is this! How
       say you?
'Tis true, my brother's daughter's Queen of Tunis;
So is she heir of Naples; 'twixt which regions
There is some space.

285 **Antonio**   A space whose every cubit
Seems to cry out, 'How shall that Claribel
Measure us back to Naples? Keep in Tunis,
And let Sebastian wake.' Say this were death
That now hath seized them; why, they were no worse
290 Than now they are. There be that can rule Naples
As well as he that sleeps; lords that can prate
As amply and unnecessarily
As this Gonzalo; I myself could make
A chough of as deep chat. O, that you bore
295 The mind that I do! What a sleep were this
For your advancement! Do you understand me?

Sebastian Methinks I do.

Antonio   And how does your content
Tender your own good fortune?

300 **Sebastian**   I remember
You did supplant your brother Prospero.

Antonio   True:
And look how well my garments sit upon me;
Much feater than before: my brother's servants
305 Were then my fellows; now they are my men.

Sebastian But for your conscience.

swallowed up by the sea—although some who were swallowed were cast out again, for they are destined to perform a drama. What's past is the opening prologue of that drama. What's still to come of that drama is yours and mine to perform.

Sebastian What stuff is this! What are you saying? It's true, my brother's daughter is Queen of Tunis. And she's the heir of Naples. And between the two places there is a great distance.

Antonio A distance whose every inch seems to cry out, "How can Claribel travel us back to Naples? Stay in Tunis and let Sebastian awaken to fortune!" [*Referring to the sleepers*] Suppose that they had just been taken by death. They would be no worse off than they are now. There are those who can rule Naples as well as this one who's sleeping here. There are lords who can prattle on and on, and just as unnecessarily, as this Gonzalo. I myself could teach a jackdaw to speak with as much wisdom as he does. Oh, if you were only of the same mind as I am! What a sleep this would be for your advancement! Do you understand what I'm saying?

Sebastian I think I do.

Antonio And how are you inclined to think about this good fortune?

Sebastian I remember that you displaced your brother, Prospero.

Antonio True. And look how well my clothing suits me now—much more gracefully than before. My brother's servants were my equals then. Now they're my servants.

Sebastian But your conscience.

Antonio Ay, sir; where lies that? if 'twere a kibe,
'Twould put me to my slipper; but I feel not
This deity in my bosom: twenty consciences,
310   That stand 'twixt me and Milan, candied be they,
And melt, ere they molest! Here lies your brother,
No better than the earth he lies upon,
If he were that which now he's like, that's dead;
Whom I, with this obedient steel, three inches of it,
315   Can lay to bed for ever; whiles you, doing thus,
To the perpetual wink for aye might put
This ancient morsel, this Sir Prudence, who
Should not upbraid our course. For all the rest,
They'll take suggestion as a cat laps milk;
320   They'll tell the clock to any business that
We say befits the hour.

Sebastian   Thy case, dear friend,
Shall be my precedent; as thou got'st Milan,
I'll come by Naples. Draw thy sword; one stroke
325   Shall free thee from the tribute which thou payest;
And I the King shall love thee.

Antonio   Draw together;
And when I rear my hand, do you the like,
To fall it on Gonzalo.

330 **Sebastian**   O, but one word.

[*They talk apart*]

[*Enter **Ariel,** with music and song*]

Ariel My master through his Art foresees the danger
That you, his friend, are in; and sends me forth –
For else his project dies – to keep them living.

[*He sings in **Gonzalo's** ear*]

Antonio   Yes, sir, and where is that? If it were a sore on my foot it would force me to put on a slipper. But I don't feel this divine thing in my heart. Twenty consciences that stood between the dukedom of Milan and me would be like sugar and melt before they bothered me. Here lies your brother. If he were what he looks like now—dead—he'd be no better than the earth upon which he lies. [*Indicating his sword*] With three inches of this obedient steel, I can lay him to bed forever. You, doing the same, might put to perpetual sleep this ancient creature, this Sir Prudence who would criticize our actions. As for the rest of them, they'll take our suggestion as a cat laps milk. They'll agree with whatever we say—keep time to any business that we say fits the hour.

Sebastian   Your situation, dear friend, shall be my example. As you got Milan, I'll get Naples. Draw your sword. One stroke will free you from the annual tribute you must pay, and I, the King, will love you for it.

Antonio   Let's both draw at the same time. When I raise my hand, you do the same, and let it fall on Gonzalo.

Sebastian   Oh, but one more word.

[*They talk privately.* **Ariel** *enters, with music and song*]

Ariel   My master, through his magic art, foresees the danger that you, his friend, are in. He sends me here to keep them living, or else his project will die.

[*He sings in* **Gonzalo's** *ear*]

> While you here do snoring lie,
335   Open-ey'd conspiracy
>   His time doth take.
> If of life you keep a care,
> Shake off slumber, and beware:
>   Awake, awake!

340   **Antonio** Then let us both be sudden.

Gonzalo [*waking*]   Now, good angels
  Preserve the King!

[*The others wake*]

Alonso   Why, how now? Ho; awake? Why are you drawn?
  Wherefore this ghastly looking?

345   **Gonzalo**   What's the matter?

Sebastian   Whiles we stood here securing your repose,
  Even now, we heard a hollow burst of bellowing
  Like bulls, or rather lions; did't not wake you?
  It struck mine ear most terribly.

350   **Alonso**   I heard nothing.

Antonio   O, 'twas a din to fright a monster's ear,
  To make an earthquake! Sure, it was the roar
  Of a whole herd of lions.

Alonso   Heard you this, Gonzalo?

355   **Gonzalo**   Upon mine honour, sir, I heard a humming,
  And that a strange one too, which did awake me:
  I shaked you, sir, and cried; as mine eyes opened,
  I saw their weapons drawn: there was a noise,
  That's verily. 'Tis best we stand upon our guard,
360   Or that we quit this place. Let's draw our weapons.

Alonso   Lead off this ground; and let's make furthur search
  For my poor son.

While you here do snoring lie,
Open-eyed conspiracy
*   His opportunity takes.*
If of life you have a care
Shake off slumber, and beware:
*   Awake, awake!*

Antonio   Then let us both be sudden.

Gonzalo   [*waking*] Now, good angels preserve the King!

[*The others awake*]

Alonso   Why, what's this? Ho! Is everyone awake? Why is your sword drawn? Why do you have such a ghastly look?

Gonzalo   What's the matter?

Sebastian   While we stood here keeping you secure as you slept, we just now heard a hollow burst of bellowing like bulls or, rather, lions. Didn't it wake you? It sounded terrible.

Alonso   I heard nothing.

Antonio   Oh, the noise was loud enough to frighten a monster or to make an earthquake! Surely, it was the roar of a whole herd of lions.

Alonso   Did you hear this, Gonzalo?

Gonzalo   Upon my honor, sir, I hear a humming, and a strange one too, which woke me. I shook you, sir, and cried out. As my eyes opened, I saw their weapons drawn. There was a noise, that's for sure. It's best we stay on guard or that we leave this place. Let's draw our weapons.

Alonso   Lead us from this ground, and let's search further for my poor son.

Gonzalo   Heavens keep him from these beasts!
    For he is, sure, i' th' island.

365 **Alonso**   Lead away.

Ariel Prospero my lord shall know what I have done:
    So, King, go safely on to seek thy son.

[Exeunt]

Gonzalo Heavens keep him from these beasts! For he is on the island, surely.

Alonso Lead away.

Ariel My lord Prospero shall know what I have done. So, King, go safely on to seek your son.

[*They exit*]

Act II

Scene II

Another part of the Island. Enter **Caliban,** *with a burthen of wood. A noise of thunder heard*

Caliban All the infections that the sun sucks up
From bogs, fens, flats, on Prosper fall, and make him
By inch-meal a disease! His spirits hear me,
And yet I needs must curse. But they'll nor pinch,
5 Fright me with urchin-shows, pitch me i' th' mire,
Nor lead me, like a firebrand, in the dark
Out of my way, unless he bid 'em: but
For every trifle are they set upon me;
Sometime like apes, that mow and chatter at me,
10 And after bite me; then like hedgehogs, which
Lie tumbling in my barefoot way, and mount
Their pricks at my footfall; sometime am I
All wound with adders, who with cloven tongues
Do hiss me into madness.

[*Enter* **Trinculo**]

15   Lo, now, lo!
Here comes a spirit of his, and to torment me
For bringing wood in slowly. I'll fall flat;
Perchance he will not mind me.

Another part of the island. **Caliban** *enters, carrying a load of wood. Thunder is heard.*

Caliban May all the infections that the sun sucks up from bogs, marshes, and swamps fall on Prospero, making him diseased inch by inch. His spirits can hear me, but I have to curse. But they won't pinch me, or frighten me with goblins, or throw me in the mud, or lead me astray in the dark in the shape of a will-o'-the-wisp, unless he tells them to. But he sets them upon me for every little thing. Sometimes they look like apes, and make faces and chatter at me, and then bite me. Then they look like hedgehogs that lie tumbled up in my path as I walk barefoot, and they raise their spines when I step on them. Sometimes snakes are all twined around me. They hiss at me with their forked tongues until I'm mad.

[**Trinculo** *enters*]

Look, now, look! Here comes a spirit of his to torment me for bringing the wood too slowly. I'll lie flat. Maybe he won't notice me.

Trinculo Here's neither bush nor shrub, to bear off any
20   weather at all, and another storm brewing; I hear it sing i' th'
wind. Yond same black cloud, yond huge one, looks like a
foul bombard that would shed his liquor. If it should
thunder as it did before, I know not where to hide my head:
yond same cloud cannot choose but fall by pailfuls. What
25   have we here? A man or a fish? Dead or alive? A fish: he
smells like a fish; a very ancient and fish-like smell; a kind
of, not of the newest Poor-John. A strange fish! Were I in
England now, as once I was, and had but this painted, not
a holiday fool there but would give a piece of silver: there
30   would this monster make a man; any strange beast there
makes a man; when they will not give a doit to relieve a lame
beggar, they will lay out ten to see a dead Indian. Legged
like a man! And his fins like arms! Warm o' my troth! I do
now let loose my opinion, hold it no longer: this is no fish,
35   but an islander, that hath lately suffered by a thunderbolt.
[*Thunder*] Alas, the storm is come again! My best way is to
creep under his gaberdine; there is no other shelter hereabout;
misery acquaints a man with strange bed-fellows. I will here
shroud till the dregs of the storm be past.

[*Enter* **Stephano,** *singing, with a bottle in his hand*]

40   **Stephano**   *I shall no more to sea, to sea,*
                    Here shall I die ashore –
This is a very scurvy tune to sing at a man's funeral; well,
here's my comfort. [*He drinks*]

              [*Sings*]

              The master, the swabber, the boatswain, and I,
45   *the gunner, and his mate,*
         Lov'd Mall, Meg, and Marian, and Margery,
                  But none of us cared for Kate;
                  For she had a tongue with a tang,

Trinculo   There isn't a bush or a shrub here to keep off the
weather at all. Another storm is brewing. I hear it sing in the
wind. That black cloud yonder—the huge one—looks like a
foul leather bottle that will split open and spill his liquor. If it
should thunder like it did before, I don't know where I'll hide
my head. That cloud yonder can't help but rain by pailfuls.
What do we have here? A man or a fish? Dead or alive? A
fish—he smells like a fish, a very ancient and fish-like smell.
A kind of not-so-fresh cheap, dried fish. A strange fish! If I
were in England now, as I once was, and if I painted a sign
there advertising this fish, every holiday fool would give me
a piece of silver to see it. There this monster would make a
man's fortune. There, any strange beast makes a man a
fortune. They won't give a little coin to relieve a lame beggar,
but they'll lay out ten to see a dead Indian. It has legs like a
man. And his fins are like arms. Warm, by my faith! I change
my opinion, and I hold it no longer. This is no fish, but an
islander who has been struck by a thunderbolt. [*Thunder*]
Alas, the storm's come again! My best bet is to creep under
his cloak. There's no other shelter around here. Misery makes
a man have strange bedfellows. I'll stay here under this
shroud until the dregs of the storm are past.

[**Stephano** *enters, singing, with a bottle in his hand*]

Stephano   *I shall no more to sea, to sea,*
               Here shall I die, ashore—

This is a very scummy song to sing at a man's funeral. Well,
here's my comfort! [*He drinks, then sings*]

   The master, the deckhand, the boatswain, and I,
       The gunner, and his mate,
   Loved Mall, Meg, and Marian, and Margery,
       But none of us cared for Kate;
       For she had a tongue with a tang,

> *Would cry to a sailor, Go hang!*
> 50   *She loved not the savour of tar nor of pitch;*
> *Yet a tailor might scratch her where'er she did itch.*
> *Then to sea, boys, and let her go hang!*

This is a scurvy tune too: but here's my comfort. [*He drinks*]

Caliban   Do not torment me: O!

55 **Stephano**   What's the matter? Have we devils here? Do you put tricks upon's with salvages and men of Ind, ha? I have not scaped drowning, to be afeard now of your four legs; for it hath been said: As proper a man as ever went on four legs cannot make him give ground; and it shall be said so again,
60   while Stephano breathes at nostrils.

Caliban   The spirit torments me: O!

Stephano   This is some monster of the isle with four legs, who hath got, as I take it, an ague. Where the devil should he learn our language? I will give him some relief, if it be
65   but for that. If I can recover him, and keep him tame, and get to Naples with him, he's a present for any emperor that ever trod on neat's-leather.

Caliban   Do not torment me, prithee; I'll bring my wood home faster.

70 **Stephano**   He's in his fit now, and does not talk after the wisest. He shall taste of my bottle; if he have never drunk wine afore, it will go near to remove his fit. If I can recover him, and keep him tame, I will not take too much for him; he shall pay for him that hath him and that soundly.

75 **Caliban**   Thou dost me yet but little hurt; thou wilt anon, I know it by thy trembling: now Prosper works upon thee.

Stephano   Come on your ways; open your mouth; here is that which will give language to you, cat. Open your mouth; this will shake your shaking, I can tell you, and that soundly: you
80   cannot tell who's your friend: open your chaps again.

She'd cry to a sailor, Go hang!
She loved not the odor of tar nor of pitch;
Yet a tailor might scratch her wherever she'd itch.
Then to sea, boys, and let her go hang!

This is a scummy tune, too. But here's my comfort. [*He drinks*]

Caliban Don't torment me! Oh!

Stephano What's the matter? Do we have devils here? Do you trick us, like a freak show with savages and men of India, heh? I haven't escaped drowning to be afraid now of your four legs. As the saying goes, "As handsome a man as ever went on four legs can't make this man run." And it'll be said again, as long as Stephano breathes.

Caliban This spirit torments me! Oh!

Stephano This is some four-legged monster of this island who has a fever, as I would guess. Where the devil did he learn our language? I'll give him some medicine, if that's what's wrong. If I can help him recover, I'll keep him tame and take him to Naples. He's a present for any emperor who ever walked on shoe-leather.

Caliban Don't torment me, please. I'll bring my wood home faster.

Stephano He's in a fit now and doesn't talk sense. I'll give him a taste from my bottle. If he's never drunk wine before, it will help cure his fit. If I can help him recover and keep him tame, I won't take *too* much for him—just be sure that whoever wants him will pay plenty for him.

Caliban You haven't yet hurt me. But you will soon. I know it by the way you're trembling. Prospero is working on you.

Stephano Come on. Open your mouth. Here's something that will make you talk—liquor makes a cat talk. Open your mouth. This will keep you from shaking, I can tell you. You can't tell that I'm your friend. Open your mouth again.

Trinculo I should know that voice: it should be – but he is
drowned; and these are devils – O defend me!

Stephano Four legs and two voices, – a most delicate
monster! His forward voice, now, is to speak well of his
85 friend; his backward voice is to utter foul speeches and to
detract. If all the wine in my bottle will recover him, I will
help his ague. Come – Amen! I will pour some in thy other
mouth.

Trinculo Stephano!

90 **Stephano** Doth thy other mouth call me? Mercy, mercy! This
is a devil, and no monster: I will leave him; I have no long
spoon.

Trinculo Stephano! If thou beest Stephano, touch me, and
speak to me; For I am Trinculo – be not afeard – thy good
95 friend Trinculo.

Stephano If thou beest Trinculo, come forth: I'll pull thee by
the lesser legs: if any be Trinculo's legs, these are they. Thou
art very Trinculo indeed! How cam'st thou to be the seige of
this moon-calf? Can he vent Trinculos?

100 **Trinculo** I took him to be killed with a thunder-stroke. But
art thou not drowned, Stephano? I hope, now, thou art not
drowned. Is the storm over-blown? I hid me under the dead
moon-calf's gaberdine for fear of the storm. And art thou
living, Stephano? O Stephano, two Neapolitans 'scaped!

105 **Stephano** Prithee, do not turn me about; my stomach is not
constant.

Caliban [*Aside*] These be fine things, an if they be not sprites.
That's a brave god, and bears celestial liquor: I will kneel to
him.

Trinculo [*from under* **Caliban***'s cloak*] I should know that voice. It should be—but he's drowned. And these are devils! Oh, help me!

Stephano Four legs and two voices—a most ingenious monster! His front voice, now, is to speak well of his friend. His back voice is to utter foul speeches and insults. If all the wine in my bottle will help him recover, I'll cure his fever. Come. Amen! I'll pour some in your other mouth.

Trinculo Stephano!

Stephano Does your other mouth call me? Mercy, mercy! This is a devil, not a monster. I'll leave him. I don't have a long spoon to eat with the devil.

Trinculo Stephano! If you are Stephano, touch me, and speak to me. For I'm Trinculo—don't be afraid—your good friend Trinculo!

Stephano If you're Trinculo, come out. I'll pull you by the smaller legs. If any are Trinculo's legs, these are the ones. You are indeed Trinculo! How did you come to be the excrement of this misshapen creature? Can he emit Trinculos?

Trinculo I took him to be killed with a thunderbolt. But aren't you drowned, Stephano? I hope, now, you aren't drowned. Is the storm blown over? I hid under the dead monster's cloak for fear of the storm. Are you really living, Stephano? Oh Stephano! Two men of Naples have escaped!

Stephano Please, don't turn me round. My stomach's upset.

Caliban [*to himself*] These are fine creatures, if they're not spirits. That's a gallant god, and he has heavenly liquor. I'll kneel to him.

110 **Stephano** How didst thou 'scape? How cam'st thou hither? Swear, by this bottle, how thou cam'st hither. I escaped upon a butt of sack, which the sailors heaved o'erboard, by this bottle! which I made of the bark of a tree with mine own hands, since I was cast ashore.

115 **Caliban** I'll swear, upon that bottle, to be thy true subject; for the liquor is not earthly.

Stephano Here; swear, then, how thou escap'dst.

Trinculo Swum ashore, man, like a duck: I can swim like a duck, I'll be sworn.

120 **Stephano** Here, kiss the book. Though thou canst swim like a duck, thou art made like a goose.

Trinculo O Stephano, hast any more of this?

Stephano The whole butt, man: my cellar is in a rock by th' sea-side, where my wine is hid. How now, moon-calf! How 125 does thine ague?

Caliban Hast thou not dropped from heaven?

Stephano Out o' the moon, I do assure thee: I was the man i' th' moon when time was.

Caliban I have seen thee in her, and I do adore thee. My 130 mistress showed me thee, and thy dog, and thy bush.

Stephano Come, swear to that; kiss the book: I will furnish it anon with new contents: swear.

Trinculo By this good light, this is a very shallow monster; I afeard of him? A very weak monster! The man i' th' moon! 135 A most credulous monster! Well drawn, monster, in good sooth!

Caliban I'll show thee every fertile inch o' th' island: and I will kiss thy foot. I prithee, be my god.

Stephano How did you escape? How did you come here? Swear by this bottle how you came here. I escaped upon a barrel of wine the sailors threw overboard—by this bottle! I made it from the bark of a tree with my hands after I was cast ashore.

Caliban I'll swear upon that bottle to be your true subject. For this liquor is not earthly.

Stephano Here. Swear, then, how you escaped.

Trinculo I swam ashore, man, like a duck. I can swim like a duck, I'll swear.

Stephano Here, take a drink. You may swim like a duck, but you're made like a goose.

Trinculo Oh, Stephano, do you have any more of this?

Stephano The whole barrel, man. My cellar is in a rock by the seaside, where my wine is hid. How now, monster! How's your fever?

Caliban Have you dropped from heaven?

Stephano Out of the moon, I assure you. I was the Man in the Moon at one time.

Caliban I've seen you in her, and I do adore you. My mistress showed you to me, and she showed me your dog and your bush.

Stephano Come swear to that. [*Giving* **Caliban** *the bottle*] Kiss the "book" and I'll fill it up again with more contents. Swear!

Trinculo By my light, this isn't much of a monster. I afraid of him? A very weak monster! The man in the moon! A very stupid monster! That's a good drink you've taken, monster, in truth.

Caliban I'll show you every fertile inch of this island. I'll kiss your foot. I pray, be my god.

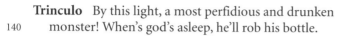

Trinculo   By this light, a most perfidious and drunken
140   monster! When's god's asleep, he'll rob his bottle.

Caliban   I'll kiss thy foot; I'll swear myself thy subject.

Stephano   Come on, then; down, and swear.

Trinculo   I shall laugh myself to death at this puppy-headed
      monster. A most scurvy monster! I could find in my heart to
145   beat him –

Stephano   Come, kiss.

Trinculo   But that the poor monster's in drink. An
      abominable monster!

Caliban   I'll show thee the best springs; I'll pluck thee berries;
150   I'll fish for thee, and get thee wood enough.
      A plague upon the tyrant that I serve!
      I'll bear him no more sticks, but follow thee,
      Thou wondrous man.

Trinculo   A most ridiculous monster, to make a wonder of a
155   poor drunkard!

Caliban   I prithee, let me bring thee where crabs grow;
      And I with my long nails will dig thee pig-nuts;
      Show thee a jay's nest, and instruct thee how
      To snare the nimble marmoset; I'll bring thee
160   To clustering filberts, and sometimes I'll get thee
      Young scamels from the rock. Wilt thou go with me?

Stephano   I prithee now, lead the way, without any more
      talking. Trinculo, the King and all our company else being
      drowned, we will inherit here. Here; bear my bottle. Fellow
165   Trinculo, we'll fill him by and by again.

Caliban   [*sings drunkenly*]   Farewell, master; farewell, farewell!

Trinculo   A howling monster; a drunken monster!

Trinculo By my light, a most treacherous and drunken monster! When his god's asleep, he'll rob the god's bottle.

Caliban I'll kiss your foot. I'll swear to be your subject.

Stephano Come on then. Down, and swear.

Trinculo I'll laugh myself to death at this simple-minded monster. A most vile monster. I could beat him—

Stephano Come, kiss.

Trinculo But the poor monster's drunk. An abominable monster!

Caliban I'll show you the best springs. I'll pluck berries for you. I'll fish for you, and get you wood. A plague upon the tyrant that I serve! I'll carry no more wood to him. But I'll follow you, you wonderful man!

Trinculo A most ridiculous monster, to be amazed by a poor drunkard!

Caliban I pray, let me show you where apples grow. I'll dig you peanuts with my long nails. I'll show you a jay's nest and teach you how to snare the nimble little monkey. I'll bring you to clusters of nuts, and sometimes I'll get you young seagulls from the rocks. Will you go with me?

Stephano I pray now, lead the way, without any more talking. [*To* **Trinculo**] Trinculo, with the King and all the rest of our company drowned, we'll inherit this place. [*To* **Caliban**] Here, carry my bottle. [*To* **Trinculo**] Trinculo, my fellow, we'll fill it again soon.

Caliban [*singing drunkenly*] Farewell, master, farewell! Farewell!

Trinculo A howling monster! A drunken monster!

Caliban [*singing*]
> *No more dams I'll make for fish;*
> > *Nor fetch in firing*
170 > > *At requiring;*
> *Nor scrape trenchering, nor wash dish:*
> > *'Ban, 'Ban, Cacaliban*
> *Has a new master – get a new man.*

Freedom, high-day! high-day, freedom! freedom, high-day,
175   freedom!

Stephano O brave monster! Lead the way.

[*Exeunt*]

Caliban   [*singing*]
   I'll make no more dams for fish;
      Nor fetch in kindling
      At his requiring;
   Nor scrape his plates, nor wash his dish;
      'Ban, 'Ban, Cacaliban
   Has a new master—Get a new man.

Freedom, high-day! High-day, freedom! Freedom, high-day, freedom!

Stephano   Oh brave monster! Lead the way.

[*They exit*]

Comprehension Check What You Know

1. Who is Alonso? Who is traveling with him?

2. Where had these characters planned to go? What set them off course? How did they end up on the island?

3. Why is Alonso unhappy? Why does he regret his daughter's marriage to the King of Tunis?

4. Why do some of the characters fall asleep in Scene 1?

5. What do Sebastian and Antonio have in common? What does Sebastian plan to do?

6. Who is Claribel?

7. What message does Ariel sing into Gonzalo's ear?

8. Who does Caliban meet in Scene 2?

9. What does Caliban complain about at the beginning of Scene 2? At the end of Act 2, what does Caliban proclaim?

Activities & Role-Playing Classes or Informal Groups

Things That Must Be Close at Hand Write a props list for Act 2. Search for clues in the text of the play. Look for stage directions in the text that list props. Study how the characters move and imagine the settings of the scenes. Add items that you think the characters might use or need to perform the scenes.

©Shakespeare & Company.

Lost and Wandering Take the roles of Alonso, Sebastian, Antonio, and Gonzalo in Scene 1. (Skip Adrian's and Francisco's lines.) Role-play the fine emotions that are "underneath" their lines. What might these characters be thinking about in the "silent" periods? Be sure to include the physical behavior of the characters. Imagine they are tired and confused. What facial expressions might Alonso show at the beginning of Scene 1? How might Gonzalo appear when he explains his vision of the island?

Discussion   Classes, Groups, or Book Clubs

1. Gonzalo says: "Had I plantation of this isle, my lord," (line 149) and "And were the King on 't, what would I do?" (line 152). Discuss how he imagines the island if he were king (lines 154–163; lines 167–172). Do you agree or disagree with his vision? Why or why not?

2. What do you think of Caliban's nature by the end of Act 2? What do his outcry and worship of Stephano tell you about Caliban?

3. Is there any harmony on the island? What order has been upset? Which characters are responsible for the harmony or the disorder? Why do you think so?

Suggestions for Writing   Improve Your Skills

1. Study the character of Ariel. Do you think Ariel is male, female, or neither? Write a paragraph including details from Acts 1 and 2 to explain your opinion.

2. Add more information to the character descriptions you wrote for Act 1. Then write character descriptions for any new characters introduced in this act.

3. Write production notes for the characters of Caliban and Alonso. List any thoughts or emotions that you think might be helpful for actors playing these parts. For example, is Alonso nervous, angry, or sad? How might he feel about being on the island?

All the World's a Stage   Introduction

Strange worlds make strange partners. Wandering through the island landscape, Shakespeare's characters are making new alliances. Some are forming conspiracies. Some are falling in love. One is a king, another believes he is a king, and still more are plotting to become kings!

Behind it all stands Prospero. With Ariel's aid, he keeps a watchful eye on all this action. Through his magic, he seems to manipulate the other characters easily, as if he were a godlike puppet master. But will he be able to keep control? Love, grief, and revenge deepen in Act 3 as Prospero shapes his plans.

What's in a Name?   Characters

In Act 2, Ferdinand and Miranda fell in love at first sight. In Act 3, they'll prove that opposites attract. Although Miranda's father is the rightful Duke of Milan, she remembers little from the world of Italian nobility. Ferdinand, on the other hand, has lived all his life as the Prince of Naples. He is well acquainted with a life of privilege and power.

To win Miranda, Ferdinand will have to behave nobly under conditions that might drive other characters to violence. He'll have to be a perfect gentleman, but he'll also have to be a servant to Prospero. We have already seen some other servants—Caliban, Trinculo, and Stephano—behave very badly indeed. Even Ariel has complained that he's not free. How well will Ferdinand stand up to this test? How good a master is Prospero?

COME WHAT MAY   Things to Watch For

How well can you picture Prospero's island? How it looks might depend on your mood or on what kind of person you are. At least, that's the case for Shakespeare's characters! It can sometimes be hard to get a handle on the island's geography because the people on it seem to view and experience it in such very different ways. As you read, look for ways in which the natural world seems to harmonize with human emotions or human nature in *The Tempest*. You have seen this before, when at the beginning of Act 2, Gonzalo saw a lush, fresh environment, while Sebastian and Antonio saw a parched area that smelled like a bog.

All Our Yesterdays   Historical and Social Context

What kind of creature is Caliban? He has been called a monster, a "moon-calf," a fish, the son of a witch and a devil, and a savage. Many stage productions have portrayed him as a fantastic creature that is part-man, part-beast. Other productions have shown Caliban to be a human—but one who looks so different to the other characters that they can't see him or treat him as a man. For example, they might cast the part to show that Caliban seems like a "monster" to the others because he's of a different race or ethnicity.

When Europeans landed on far shores, they found people who looked very different from them. They encountered strange animals they had never seen before. They sometimes heard stories about even stranger creatures from the local inhabitants or from other travelers. Columbus, for example, recorded stories in his notebook about one-eyed men and men with dogs' muzzles in the New World. Scientific and reference texts used throughout the Middle Ages occasionally told of strange monster-men or fantastic beasts in remote locations.

The Play's the Thing Staging

The Tempest is full of stage directions—many more than are usually found in Shakespeare's plays. We aren't sure why this is the case. It's possible that Shakespeare didn't write them at all, but that they were added later by someone else. Some scholars have also suggested that Shakespeare wrote *The Tempest* at home in Stratford, rather than in London, where the play was performed. In that case, he would have had to write precise directions on the page because he could not work them out with his company during rehearsals.

One stage direction is quite mysterious. In Act 3, the stage directions tell us that a "quaint device" will allow an object to vanish magically from the stage. What was this "quaint device"? Perhaps it was some tricky distraction or use of stage machinery that made things seem to disappear.

My Words Fly Up Language

Caliban's name is probably a rearrangement of the letters in the word *cannibal*. In *The Tempest*, Caliban is "natural" in more ways than one. When Trinculo calls him "a natural" in Act 3's Scene 2, it's no compliment. Trinculo is calling Caliban an idiot.

Other exotic creatures mentioned in Act 3 come from myth. A *harpy* is a wind spirit with the face of a woman and the body of a bird. In Greek and Roman mythology, harpies are often disgusting creatures who torture and harass humans. The *phoenix* originated in Egyptian mythology. This fabulous mythical bird lived for at least 500 years, then set its nest on fire. A new phoenix miraculously rose from the ashes to live another long age. Since only one bird could live at a time, the phoenix was said to be "reborn" with each new age.

Act III

Scene I

Before Prospero's Cell. Enter **Ferdinand,** *bearing a log*

Ferdinand   There be some sports are painful, and their labour
Delight in them sets off: some kinds of baseness
Are nobly undergone; and most poor matters
Point to rich ends. This my mean task
5   Would be as heavy to me as odious, but
The mistress which I serve quickens what's dead,
And makes my labours pleasures. O, she is
Ten times more gentle than her father's crabbed,
And he's composed of harshness. I must remove
10   Some thousands of these logs, and pile them up,
Upon a sore injunction: my sweet mistress
Weeps when she sees me work, and says, such baseness
Had never like executor. I forget:
But these sweet thoughts do even refresh my labours,
15   Most busilest when I do it.

[*Enter* **Miranda***; and* **Prospero,** *at a distance, unseen*]

Miranda   Alas now, pray you,
Work not so hard: I would the lightning had
Burnt up those logs that you are enjoined to pile!
Pray, set it down, and rest you: when this burns,
20   'Twill weep for having wearied you. My father
Is hard at study; pray, now, rest yourself:
He's safe for these three hours.

In front of Prospero's cave. **Ferdinand** *enters, carrying a log.*

Ferdinand Some sports are difficult, but their labor is offset by the delight they give. Some kinds of menial labor can be performed with dignity. And most humble work has a worthy end. This menial task that I do could be as difficult to me as it is unpleasant. But the lady for whom I work makes it lively and makes my labor pleasurable. Oh, she's ten times gentler than her irritable father. He is nothing but harsh. I must move thousands of these logs and pile them up by his harsh command. My sweet mistress weeps when she sees me work. She says that such menial work as this was never done by someone of my quality. But I forget myself. These sweet thoughts make my labor easier, and I work hardest when I daydream like this.

[**Miranda** *enters.* **Prospero** *is at a distance, unseen*]

Miranda Alas now, please, don't work so hard. I wish that a lightning strike had burnt these logs that you've been commanded to pile up! Please, set it down and rest. When this log burns, it will weep for having made you so weary. My father is busy with his studies. Please, rest yourself. He won't bother us for the next three hours.

Ferdinand   O most dear mistress,
    The sun will set before I shall discharge
25 What I must strive to do.

  Miranda   If you'll sit down,
    I'll bear your logs the while: pray give me that;
    I'll carry it to the pile.

Ferdinand   No, precious creature;
30 I had rather crack my sinews, break my back,
    Than you should such dishonour undergo,
    While I sit lazy by.

  Miranda   It would become me
    As well as it does you: and I should do it
35 With much more ease; for my good will is to it,
    And yours it is against.

Prospero   Poor worm, thou art infected!
    This visitation shows it.

  Miranda   You look wearily.

40 **Ferdinand**   No, noble mistress: 'tis fresh morning with me
    When you are by at night. I do beseech you –
    Chiefly that I might set it in my prayers –
    What is your name?

  Miranda   Miranda. O my father,
45 I have broke your hest to say so!

  Ferdinand   Admired Miranda!
    Indeed the top of admiration! worth
    What's dearest to the world! Full many a lady
    I have eyed with best regard, and many a time
50 Th' harmony of their tongues hath into bondage
    Brought my too diligent ear: for several virtues
    Have I liked several women; never any
    With so full soul, but some defect in her

Ferdinand Oh, most dear mistress. The sun will set before I finish what I have to do.

Miranda If you'll sit down, I'll carry your logs awhile. Please, give that to me. I'll carry it to the pile.

Ferdinand No, precious creature. I'd rather tear my muscles or break my back than let you do such dishonorable work while I sit lazily by.

Miranda It would become me as well as it does you. And I would do it more easily, since I want to do it and you don't.

Prospero [*commenting unseen*] You poor thing. You're infected with love. This visit shows it.

Miranda You look tired.

Ferdinand No, noble mistress. It's like the fresh morning for me when you're nearby at night. I do beg you—mainly so that I might mention it in my prayers—what is your name?

Miranda Miranda. Oh! My father, I've broken your instructions in saying so.

Ferdinand Admired Miranda! Indeed, the highest in admiration. The most precious in the world! I've eyed many a lady with highest admiration, and many times the sweetness of their words have captured my too-attentive ear. I've liked particular women for particular qualities. But never has anyone been so perfect that some defect in her

Did quarrel with the noblest grace she owed,
55   And put it to the foil: but you, O you,
So perfect and so peerless, are created
Of every creature's best!

Miranda   I do not know
One of my sex; no woman's face remember,
60   Save, from my glass, mine own; nor have I seen
More that I may call men than you, good friend,
And my dear father: how features are abroad,
I am skilless of; but, by my modesty,
The jewel in my dower, I would not wish
65   Any companion in the world but you;
Nor can imagination form a shape,
Besides yourself, to like of. But I prattle
Something too wildly, and my father's precepts
I therein do forget.

70 **Ferdinand**   I am, in my condition,
A prince, Miranda; I do think, a King –
I would not so – and would no more endure
This wooden slavery than to suffer
The flesh-fly blow my mouth. Hear my soul speak:
75   The very instant that I saw you, did
My heart fly to your service; there resides,
To make me slave to it; and for your sake
Am I this patient log-man.

Miranda   Do you love me?

80 **Ferdinand**   O heaven, O earth, bear witness to this sound,
And crown what I profess with kind event,
If I speak true! If hollowly, invert
What best is boded me to mischief! I,
Beyond all limit of what else i' th' world,
85   Do love, prize, honour you.

Miranda   I am a fool
To weep at what I am glad of.

did not seem to quarrel with the noble grace in her and defeat it. But you! Oh you! So perfect and without equal. You are made of every other one's best virtues.

Miranda I don't know another woman. I don't remember another woman's face, except my own I see in my mirror. Nor have I seen any other man than you, good friend, and my dear father. I have no knowledge of what people elsewhere look like. But by my modesty—the jewel of my possessions— I wouldn't wish any companion in the world but you. Nor can I imagine anyone besides yourself that I like so well. But I talk too wildly and forget my father's instructions.

Ferdinand I am, in rank, a prince, Miranda. I think that perhaps I am a king, although I wish it weren't so. So I would no more endure this wood-lugging slavery that I would allow a blowfly to defile my mouth. Hear my soul speak: The instant I saw you, my heart flew to your service. And there it stays. I am a slave to you. And for your sake I am this patient log-man.

Miranda Do you love me?

Ferdinand Oh heaven! Oh earth! Bear witness to what I say, and if I speak the truth, crown my vows with success. If I speak falsely, turn all my good fortune to misfortune. I— beyond the limit of anything else in the world—do love, prize, and honor you.

Miranda I'm a fool to weep at what I'm so happy about.

Prospero   Fair encounter
        Of two most rare affections! Heavens rain grace
90   On that which breeds between 'em!

Ferdinand   Wherefore weep you?

Miranda At mine unworthiness, that dare not offer
        What I desire to give; and much less take
        What I shall die to want. But this is trifling;
95   And all the more it seeks to hide itself,
        The bigger bulk it shows. Hence, bashful cunning!
        And prompt me plain and holy innocence!
        I am your wife if you will marry me;
        If not, I'll die your maid: to be your fellow
100   You may deny me; but I'll be your servant,
        Whether you will or no.

Ferdinand   My mistress, dearest;
        And I thus humble ever.

Miranda   My husband, then?

105 **Ferdinand** Ay, with a heart as willing
        As bondage e'er of freedom: here's my hand.

Miranda And mine, with my heart in 't: and now farewell
        Till half an hour hence.

Ferdinand   A thousand thousand!

[*Exeunt* **Ferdinand** *and* **Miranda**, *severally*]

110 **Prospero** So glad of this as they I cannot be,
        Who are surprised with all; but my rejoicing
        At nothing can be more. I'll to my book;
        For yet, ere supper-time, must I perform
        Much business appertaining.

[*Exit*]

Prospero [*unseen*] A happy meeting of two rare souls. May the heavens bless their union.

Ferdinand Why do you weep?

Miranda At my unworthiness. I don't dare offer what I wish to give, much less take what I will die without. But this is nonsense. The more I try to hide the truth, the more it shows itself. No more bashful coyness. Let me speak the plain and innocent truth: I will be your wife if you will marry me. If not, I'll die your servant. You may refuse me as your mate, but I'll be your servant whether you wish it or not.

Ferdinand My wife, dearest! And I am humbly yours forever.

Miranda My husband then?

Ferdinand Yes, with a heart as willing as ever slavery wishes freedom: Here's my hand.

Miranda And mine, with my heart in it. And now farewell till half an hour from now.

Ferdinand A thousand thousand farewells!

[**Ferdinand** *and* **Miranda** *exit separately*]

Prospero I can't be as glad of this as they are, because they're surprised by it all. But nothing could cause me more rejoicing. I'll get back to my book, since before suppertime I have much business to do.

[**Prospero** *exits*]

Act III

Scene II

Another part of the Island. Enter **Caliban, Stephano** *and* **Trinculo**

Stephano Tell not me – when the butt is out, we will drink water; not a drop before: therefore bear up, and board 'em. Servant-monster, drink to me.

Trinculo Servant-monster! The folly of this island! They say
5   there's but five upon this isle: we are three of them; if th' other two be brained like us, the state totters.

Stephano Drink, servant-monster, when I bid thee: thy eyes are almost set in thy head.

Trinculo Where should they be set else? He were a brave
10   monster indeed, if they were set in his tail.

Stephano My man-monster hath drowned his tongue in sack: for my part, the sea cannot drown me; I swam, ere I could recover the shore, five-and-thirty leagues off and on. By this light, thou shalt be my lieutenant, monster, or my standard.

15 **Trinculo** Your lieutenant, if you list; he's no standard.

Stephano We'll not run, Monsieur Monster.

Trinculo Nor go neither; but you'll lie, like dogs, and yet say nothing neither.

Stephano Moon-calf, speak once in thy life, if thou beest a
20   good moon-calf.

Another part of the island. **Caliban, Stephano,** *and* **Trinculo** *enter.*

Stephano Don't tell me. When the wine barrel is empty, we'll drink water. But not a drop before. So stand firm and attack! Servant-monster, drink to me.

Trinculo "Servant-monster"? The stupidity on this island! They say there are only five on this island, and we're three of them. If the other two are as stupid as we are, the country's in trouble!

Stephano Drink, servant-monster, when I tell you to. Your eyes are almost sunken in your head.

Trinculo Where else should they be? He would be a strange monster indeed, if they were in his tail.

Stephano My man-monster has drowned his tongue in wine. For my part, the sea can't drown me. I swam thirty-five leagues off and on before I reached the shore. By this light, you could be my lieutenant, monster, or my standard-bearer.

Trinculo Your lieutenant, if you wish. But he's no standard-bearer—he can't stand!

Stephano We won't run away from the enemy, Mr. Monster.

Trinculo You won't walk either. You'll lie there like dogs and yet say nothing.

Stephano Monster, speak for once in your life if you're a good monster.

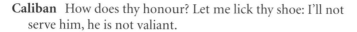

Caliban How does thy honour? Let me lick thy shoe: I'll not
serve him, he is not valiant.

Trinculo Thou liest, most ignorant monster: I am in case to
jostle a constable. Why, thou deboshed fish, thou, was there
25   ever man a coward that hath drunk so much sack as I today?
Wilt thou tell a monstrous lie, being but half a fish and half
a monster?

Caliban Lo, how he mocks me! Wilt thou let him, my lord?

Trinculo 'Lord,' quoth he? That a monster should be such a
30   natural!

Caliban Lo, lo, again! Bite him to death, I prithee.

Stephano Trinculo, keep a good tongue in your head: if you
prove a mutineer – the next tree! The poor monster's my
subject, and he shall not suffer indignity.

35   **Caliban** I thank my noble lord. Wilt thou be pleased to
hearken once again to the suit I made to thee?

Stephano Marry, will I: kneel and repeat it; I will stand, and
so shall Trinculo.

[*Enter* **Ariel,** *invisible*]

Caliban As I told thee before, I am subject to a tyrant, a
40   sorcerer, that by his cunning hath cheated me of the island.

Ariel Thou liest.

Caliban 'Thou liest,' thou jesting monkey, thou!
I would my valiant master would destroy thee!
I do not lie.

45   **Stephano** Trinculo, if you trouble him any more in 's tale, by
this hand, I will supplant some of your teeth.

Trinculo Why, I said nothing.

Caliban How are you, your honor? Let me lick your shoe. I won't serve him. He's not courageous.

Trinculo You lie, you ignorant monster! I'm courageous enough to push around a law officer. Why you drunken fish, you! Was there ever a man who was a coward who has drunk as much wine as I have today? Will you tell such a monstrous lie, you being nothing but half a fish and half a monster?

Caliban Look how he mocks me! Will you let him, my lord?

Trinculo "Lord," he said? Imagine such an unnatural monster being such a natural idiot!

Caliban Look! Look, he's done it again! Bite him to death, I beg you.

Stephano Trinculo, keep a civil tongue in your head. If you turn out to be a mutineer, you'll be hanged from the next tree! The poor monster is my subject, and I won't allow him to suffer such indignity.

Caliban I thank you, my noble lord. Will you please listen once again to the favor I asked of you?

Stephano Indeed I will! Kneel and repeat it. I will stand, and so will Trinculo.

[**Ariel** *enters, invisible*]

Caliban As I told you before, I'm subject to a tyrant, a sorcerer, who has cheated me out of this island by his cunning.

Ariel [*invisible*] *You* lie!

Caliban [*thinking he heard* **Trinculo** *speak*] *You* lie, you fool of a monkey, you! I wish my valiant master would destroy you! I do not lie!

Stephano Trinculo, if you bother him anymore while he's telling his tale, by this hand I'll knock out some of your teeth.

Trinculo Why? I said nothing!

Stephano Mum, then, and no more. Proceed.

Caliban I say, by sorcery he got this isle;
50   From me he got it. If thy greatness will
      Revenge it on him – for I know thou dar'st,
      But this thing dare not –

Stephano That's most certain.

Caliban Thou shalt be lord of it, and I'll serve thee.

55 **Stephano** How now shall this be compassed? Canst thou
      bring me to the party?

Caliban Yea, yea, my lord: I'll yield him thee asleep,
      Where thou mayst knock a nail into his head.

Ariel Thou liest; thou canst not.

60 **Caliban** What a pied ninny's this! Thou scurvy patch!
      I do beseech thy greatness, give him blows,
      And take his bottle from him: when that's gone,
      He shall drink nought but brine; for I'll not show him
      Where the quick freshes are.

65 **Stephano** Trinculo, run into no further danger: interrupt the
      monster one word further, and, by this hand, I'll turn my
      mercy out o' doors, and make a stock-fish of thee.

Trinculo Why, what did I? I did nothing. I'll go farther off.

Stephano Didst thou not say he lied?

70 **Ariel** Thou liest.

Stephano Do I so? Take thou that. [*Beats him*] As you like
      this, give me the lie another time.

Trinculo I did not give the lie. Out o' your wits, and hearing
      too? A pox o' your bottle! This can sack and drinking do. A
75   murrain on your monster, and the devil take your fingers!

Stephano Be quiet, then, and no more of this! [*To* **Caliban**]
Proceed.

Caliban I was saying that he got this island by sorcery. He got
it from me. If Your Greatness would take revenge on him—I
know you dare, but that thing over there would never dare—

Stephano That's for sure!

Caliban —you shall be the lord of it, and I'll serve you.

Stephano How can we do it? Can you take me to this person?

Caliban Yes, yes, my lord. I'll give him up to you while he's
asleep. Then you can knock a nail into his head.

Ariel You lie! You can't!

Caliban What a fool he is. You contemptible clown! I beg Your
Greatness, give him a beating and take his bottle away.
When that's gone he'll have nothing to drink but salt water,
because I won't show him where the fresh springs are.

Stephano Trinculo, stay out of trouble! Interrupt the monster
one more time and by this hand I'll show you no mercy. I'll
beat you black and blue.

Trinculo Why? What did I do? I did nothing! I'll go farther away.

Stephano Didn't you say he lied?

Ariel You lie!

Stephano I do, do I? Take that! [*Beats* **Trinculo**] If you like it,
then tell me again that I lie.

Trinculo I didn't say you lied. Are you out of your wits and lost
your hearing too? Damn your bottle! This is what wine and
drinking do. May a plague fall on your monster, and the devil
take your fingers!

Caliban Ha, ha, ha!

Stephano No, forward with your tale. Prithee, stand further
off.

Caliban Beat him enough: after a little time,
80   I'll beat him too.

Stephano   Stand farther. Come, proceed.

Caliban Why, as I told thee, 'tis a custom with him
I' th' afternoon to sleep: there thou mayst brain him,
Having first seized his books; or with a log
85   Batter his skull, or paunch him with a stake,
Or cut his wezand with thy knife. Remember
First to possess his books; for without them
He's but a sot, as I am, nor hath not
One spirit to command: they all do hate him
90   As rootedly as I. Burn but his books.
He has brave utensils – for so he calls them –
Which, when he has a house, he'll deck withal.
And that most deeply to consider is
The beauty of his daughter; he himself
95   Calls her a nonpareil: I never saw a woman,
But only Sycorax my dam and she;
But she as far surpasseth Sycorax
As great'st does least.

Stephano   Is it so brave a lass?

100 **Caliban** Ay, lord; she will become thy bed, I warrant,
And bring thee forth brave brood.

Stephano Monster, I will kill this man: his daughter and I
will be king and queen – save our graces! – and Trinculo
and thyself shall be viceroys. Dost thou like the plot,
105 Trinculo?

Trinculo Excellent.

Caliban Ha, ha, ha!

Stephano Now go on with your story. Please, stand farther away.

Caliban Beat him good. Then I'll beat him too.

Stephano Stand farther back. [*To* **Caliban**] Okay, go on.

Caliban Well, as I told you, it's his habit to sleep in the afternoon. You can knock his brains out there, after first taking his books. Or you could batter his skull with a log, or run a stake through his belly, or cut his throat with your knife. Remember, first get his books. Without them he's as much a fool as I am, without a single spirit to command. They all hate him to the bottom of their souls, just as I do. But burn just his books. He has fine furnishings, so he calls them, which he'll use to decorate his house when he has one. But above all, think about the beauty of his daughter. He himself says she is without equal. I've never seen any women except my mother Sycorax and her. But she so far surpasses Sycorax in beauty as the greatest surpasses the least.

Stephano Is she that beautiful a girl?

Caliban Yes, lord. And she'll be an asset to your bed, I promise you, and give you a fine brood of children.

Stephano Monster, I will kill this man. His daughter and I will be king and queen—God save our graces!—and Trinculo and you shall be viceroys. Do you like the plot, Trinculo?

Trinculo Excellent!

Stephano Give me thy hand: I am sorry I beat thee; but, while
thou liv'st, keep a good tongue in thy head.

Caliban Within this half hour will he be asleep:
110   Wilt thou destroy him then?

Stephano   Ay, on mine honour.

Ariel This will I tell my master.

Caliban Thou mak'st me merry; I am full of pleasure:
Let us be jocund: will you troll the catch
115   You taught me but the while-ere?

Stephano At thy request, monster, I will do reason, any
reason. Come on, Trinculo, let us sing.

[*Sings*]
Flout 'em and scout 'em,
And scout 'em and flout 'em;
120   *Thought is free.*

Caliban That's not the tune.

[**Ariel** *plays the tune on a tabor and pipe*]

Stephano What is this same?

Trinculo This is the tune of our catch, played by the picture
of Nobody.

125   **Stephano** If thou beest a man, show thyself in thy likeness: if
thou beest a devil, take 't as thou list.

Trinculo O, forgive me my sins!

Stephano He that dies pays all debts: I defy thee. Mercy upon
us!

130   **Caliban** Art thou afeard?

Stephano   No, monster, not I.

Stephano Give me your hand. I'm sorry I beat you. But from now on, keep a civil tongue in your head.

Caliban He'll be asleep within a half hour. Will you destroy him then?

Stephano I will, on my honor.

Ariel I'll tell my master this.

Caliban You make me happy! I'm so pleased! Let's have some cheer! Will you sing the tune that you taught me a while ago?

Stephano If you ask, monster, I'll do anything, anything. Come on, Trinculo. Let's sing.

> [*Sings*]
> *Sneer at 'em, jeer at 'em,*
> *Jeer at 'em, sneer at 'em,*
> *Thought is free—*

Caliban That's not the tune.

[**Ariel** *plays the tune on a drum and pipe*]

Stephano What is this?

Trinculo This is the tune of our song, played by someone invisible!

Stephano If you're a man, show yourself in your own shape! If you're a devil, take whatever shape you like!

Trinculo Oh, forgive me my sins!

Stephano He who dies pays all his debts. I defy you! Mercy on us!

Caliban Are you afraid?

Stephano No, monster, not I.

Caliban   Be not afeard; the isle is full of noises,
Sounds and sweet airs, that give delight, and hurt not.
Sometimes a thousand twangling instruments
135   Will hum about mine ears; and sometime voices,
That, if I then had wak'd after long sleep,
Will make me sleep again: and then, in dreaming,
The clouds methought would open, and show riches
Ready to drop upon me; that, when I wak'd,
140   I cried to dream again.

Stephano   This will prove a brave kingdom to me, where I
shall have my music for nothing.

Caliban   When Prospero is destroyed.

Stephano   That shall be by and by: I remember the story.

145 **Caliban**   The sound is going away; let's follow it, and after do
our work.

Stephano   Lead, monster; we'll follow I would I could see this
taborer; he lays it on. Wilt come?

Trinculo   I'll follow, Stephano.

[Exeunt]

Caliban Don't be afraid. This island is full of noises, sounds, and sweet songs, that are delightful and not harmful. Sometimes the sound of a thousand twangling instruments will hum in my ears. And sometimes voices that, if I have awakened after a long sleep, will make me sleep again. And in my dreams, clouds seem to open and show riches ready to drop into my lap. So that, when I awaken, I cry to dream again.

Stephano This promises to be a splendid kingdom for me, where I will have my music for free!

Caliban When Prospero is destroyed.

Stephano That will happen very soon. I remember your story.

Caliban The sound is going away. Let's follow it [*meaning the music*] and afterward do our work.

Stephano Lead on, monster. We'll follow. I wish I could see this drummer. He plays well. [*To* **Trinculo**] Are you coming?

Trinculo I'll follow you, Stephano.

[*They exit*]

Act III

Scene III

Another part of the Island. Enter **Alonso, Sebastian, Antonio, Gonzalo, Adrian, Francisco,** *and others*

Gonzalo By'r lakin, I can go no further, sir;
My old bones ache: here's a maze trod, indeed,
Through forth-rights and meanders! By your patience,
I needs must rest me.

5 **Alonso**   Old lord, I cannot blame thee,
Who am myself attached with weariness,
To th' dulling of my spirits: sit down, and rest.
Even here I will put off my hope, and keep it
No longer for my flatterer: he is drowned
10 Whom thus we stray to find; and the sea mocks
Our frustrate search on land. Well, let him go.

Antonio [*Aside to* **Sebastian**] I am right glad that he's so out
     of hope.
Do not, for one repulse, forego the purpose
15 That you resolved t' effect.

Sebastian [*Aside to* **Antonio**] The next advantage
Will we take throughly.

Antonio [*Aside to* **Sebastian**] Let it be to-night;
For, now they are oppressed with travel, they
20 Will not, nor cannot, use such vigilance
As when they are fresh.

Sebastian [*Aside to* **Antonio**] I say, to-night: no more.

Another part of the island. **Alonso, Sebastian, Antonio, Gonzalo, Adrian, Francisco,** *and others enter.*

Gonzalo By Our Lady, I can go no farther, sir. My old bones ache. What a maze we've walked, indeed, through straight paths and through twists and turns. With your patience, I must rest.

Alonso Old lord, I don't blame you. I myself am filled with weariness so that I can hardly move. Sit down and rest. I've about given up hope. It no longer keeps me going. My son, whom we are looking for, is drowned. The sea mocks our pointless search on land. Well, I must accept that he is gone.

Antonio [*privately to* **Sebastian**] I'm glad that he's so out of hope. Because of one failure, don't give up the plan that you've set your mind to carry out.

Sebastian [*privately to* **Antonio**] We'll take full advantage of the next chance we get.

Antonio [*privately to* **Sebastian**] Let's do it tonight. Now they're tired with travel. They won't, or can't, be as watchful as when they're fresh.

Sebastian [*privately to* **Antonio**] Okay. Tonight. Say no more.

[*Solemn and strange music;* **Prospero** *enters, invisible. Enter several strange Shapes, bringing in a banquet; they dance about it with gentle actions of salutations; inviting the King, etc. to eat, they depart*]

Alonso   What harmony is this? My good friends, hark!

Gonzalo   Marvellous sweet music!

25 **Alonso**   Give us kind keepers, heavens! What were these?

Sebastian   A living drollery. Now I will believe
That there are unicorns; that in Arabia
There is one tree, the phoenix' throne; one phoenix
At this hour reigning there.

30 **Antonio**   I'll believe both;
And what does else want credit, come to me,
And I'll be sworn 'tis true: travellers ne'er did lie,
Though fools at home condemn 'em.

Gonzalo   If in Naples
35 I should report this now, would they believe me?
If I should say, I saw such islanders –
For, certes, these are people of the island –
Who, though they are of monstrous shape, yet, note,
Their manners are more gentle, kind, than of
40 Our human generation you shall find
Many, nay, almost any.

Prospero   [*Aside*]   Honest lord,
Thou hast said well; for some of you there present
Are worse than devils.

45 **Alonso**   I cannot too much muse
Such shapes, such gesture, and such sound, expressing –
Although they want the use of tongue – a kind
Of excellent dumb discourse.

Prospero   [*Aside*]   Praise in departing.

[*Solemn and strange music plays.* **Prospero** *enters, invisible. Several strangely shaped Spirits enter, bringing a banquet. They dance around it, gently inviting* **Alonso** *and the others to eat. Then they exit*]

Alonso What music is this? My good friends, listen!

Gonzalo Marvelously sweet music!

Alonso Guardian angels protect us! What were those?

Sebastian A puppet show with live actors! Now I'll believe in unicorns. And I'll believe that in Arabia there's a tree that's a throne for the phoenix, and that at this very moment a phoenix sits on that throne.

Antonio I'll believe both. And anything else that's incredible. Ask me, and I'll swear it's true. Travelers never lie, even though fools at home accuse them of it!

Gonzalo If I would report this now in Naples, would they believe me? If I said I saw such islanders (for certainly these are people of this island) who, even though they have unnatural shapes, have manners more gentle and kind than many humans—indeed, almost any human!

Prospero [*to himself*] Honest lord. You speak the truth. For some of you there are worse than devils.

Alonso I can't help being amazed at these spirits. Without language, just with gestures and sounds, they can communicate so well. An excellent silent language!

Prospero [*to himself*] Wait until the end of their show before praising them.

50 **Francisco** They vanished strangely.

Sebastian   No matter, since
    They have left their viands behind; for we have stomachs.
    Will 't please you taste of what is here?

Alonso   Not I.

55 **Gonzalo** Faith, sir, you need not fear. When we were boys,
    Who would believe that there were mountaineers
    Dew-lapped like bulls, whose throats had hanging at 'em
    Wallets of flesh? or that there were such men
    Whose heads stood in their breasts? which now we find
60   Each putter-out of five for one will bring us
    Good warrant of.

Alonso   I will stand to, and feed,
    Although my last; no matter, since I feel
    The best is past. Brother, my lord the duke,
65   Stand to, and do as we.

[*Thunder and lightning. Enter* **Ariel** *like a Harpy; he claps*
his wings upon the table; and, with a quaint device, the ban-
quet vanishes]

Ariel You are three men of sin, whom Destiny –
    That hath to instrument this lower world
    And what is in 't – the never-surfeited sea
    Hath caused to belch up you; and on this island,
70   Where man doth not inhabit – you 'mongst men
    Being most unfit to live. I have made you mad;
    And even with such-like valour men hang and drown
    Their proper selves.

[**Alonso, Sebastian,** *etc. draw their swords*]

               You fools! I and my fellows
75   Are ministers of Fate: the elements,
    Of whom your swords are tempered, may as well
    Wound the loud winds, or with bemocked-at stabs

Francisco They've vanished strangely.

Sebastian It doesn't matter. They've left their food behind. We're hungry. Would you like to taste something here?

Alonso Not I.

Gonzalo By my faith, sir, you needn't fear. When we were boys who would have believed that there were people living in the mountains who, like bulls, had throats hanging down like purses of flesh? Or that there were men whose heads were in the middle of their chests? Which we now hear about from practically every traveler who returns from strange lands.

Alonso I'll take the risk and eat, although it may be my last meal. But that does not matter, since I feel the best of my life is past. Brother, my lord the duke, do as I do, and eat.

[*Thunder and lightning.* **Ariel** *enters in the shape of a Harpy. He spreads his wings over the table and, with an ingenious device, the banquet vanishes*]

Ariel You are three sinful men. Destiny—whose instrument is this world and everything in it—has made the always-hungry sea belch you up on this island, where no man lives. You of all men are the most unfit to live. I have made you mad. And with the fake courage of madness like yours, men hang and drown themselves.

[**Alonso, Sebastian,** *and the others draw their swords*]

You fools. I and my fellows are the ministers of Fate. We are the elements from which your swords are made. You may as well try to wound the loud winds or try to kill the seas, which

Kill the still-closing waters, as diminish
One dowl that's in my plume: my fellow-ministers
80 Are like invulnerable. If you could hurt,
Your swords are now too massy for your strengths,
And will not be uplifted. But remember –
For that's my business to you – that you three
From Milan did supplant good Prospero:
85 Exposed unto the sea, which hath requit it,
Him and his innocent child: for which foul deed
The powers, delaying, not forgetting, have
Incensed the seas and shores, yea, all the creatures,
Against your peace. Thee of thy son, Alonso,
90 They have bereft; and do pronounce by me
Ling'ring perdition – worse than any death
Can be at once – shall step by step attend
You and your ways; whose wraths to guard you from –
Which here, in this most desolate isle, else falls
95 Upon your heads – is nothing but heart-sorrow
And a clear life ensuing.

[*He vanishes in thunder; then, to soft music, enter the*
Shapes again; they dance, with mocks and mows, carrying
out the table]

Prospero   Bravely the figure of this Harpy hast thou
Performed, my Ariel; a grace it had devouring:
Of my instruction hast thou nothing bated
100 In what thou hadst to say: so, with good life
And observation strange, my meaner ministers
Their several kinds have done. My high charms work,
And these mine enemies are all knit up
In their distractions; they now are in my power;
105 And in these fits I leave them, while I visit
Young Ferdinand – whom they suppose is drowned –
And his and mine loved darling.

[*Exit*]

close at each stab. You cannot injure the smallest feather in my plume. My fellow spirits are as invulnerable as I am. Even if you could hurt us, your swords are now too heavy for your strength. You can't lift them up. But remember—and this is why I've come to you—that you three from Milan expelled good Prospero and exposed him and his innocent child to the sea, which has repaid you for it. For your foul deed the powers—delaying, but not forgetting—have caused the seas and shores and every creature to turn against you. They have taken your son from you, Alonso. And they pronounce through me that you are sentenced to lingering suffering—worse than a quick death. This suffering will follow you step by step, everywhere you go. Nothing but heartfelt sorrow and a sinless life hereafter will protect you from the wrath of these powers, which falls upon your heads here in this desolate island.

[*He vanishes with thunder. Then, to soft music, the* **Spirits** *return. They dance mockingly as they carry out the table*]

Prospero You've performed the part of this Harpy brilliantly, my Ariel, with a ravishing grace. You didn't leave out any of my instructions as you gave them your speech. My lesser spirits have played their parts convincingly and with exceptional care as well. My powerful charms have worked, and my enemies are all tangled up in confusion. Now they're in my power. I'll leave them in their fits while I visit young Ferdinand—whom they believe is drowned—and his and my beloved darling girl.

[**Prospero** *exits*]

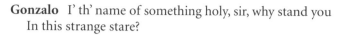

Gonzalo I' th' name of something holy, sir, why stand you
In this strange stare?

110 **Alonso**   O, it is monstrous, monstrous!
Methought the billows spoke, and told me of it;
The winds did sing it to me; and the thunder,
That deep and dreadful organ-pipe, pronounced
The name of Prosper: it did bass my trespass.
115 Therefore my son i' th' ooze is bedded; and
I'll seek him deeper than e'er plummet sounded,
And with him there lie mudded.

[*Exit*]

Sebastian   But one fiend at a time,
I'll fight their legions o'er.

120 **Antonio**   I'll be thy second.

[*Exeunt* **Sebastian** *and* **Antonio**]

Gonzalo All three of them are desperate: their great guilt,
Like poison given to work a great time after,
Now 'gins to bite the spirits. I do beseech you,
That are of suppler joints, follow them swiftly,
125 And hinder them from what this ecstasy
May now provoke them to.

Adrian   Follow, I pray you.

[*Exeunt*]

Gonzalo In the name of all that's holy, sir, why do you stand there with a strange stare?

Alonso Oh, it is monstrous, monstrous! I thought the waves spoke and told me of my sin. The winds sang it to me. And the thunder, like that deep and dreadful sound of a pipe organ, pronounced the name of Prospero. It boomed out my guilt. That's why my son sleeps in the ooze of the sea bottom! I'll seek him deeper than has ever been measured, and lie with him there in the mud.

[**Alonso** *exits*]

Sebastian Give me just one fiend at a time, and I'll fight all their legions.

Antonio I'll be your second.

[**Sebastian** *and* **Antonio** *exit*]

Gonzalo All three of them are desperate. Their great guilt, like a slow-working poison, now begins to bite their spirits. I beg you, who can move more easily, follow them quickly and keep them from harming themselves in their madness.

Adrian Follow me, please.

[*They exit*]

Comprehension Check What You Know

1. In Scene 1, what does Ferdinand tell Miranda about his past romantic experiences? What does Miranda promise to Ferdinand?

2. What plans do Caliban, Stephano, and Trinculo have for Prospero in Scene 2? How do these plans compare to Sebastian and Antonio's plot?

3. Ariel interrupts Caliban, Stephano, and Trinculo in Scene 2. Why does this add comedy? How does he trick the three at the end of the scene?

4. In Scene 3, what do you learn about Gonzalo's character from Prospero's comments about the old councilor?

5. What message does Ariel (in the form of a harpy) deliver to Alonso, Sebastian, and Antonio?

6. Describe how each character reacts to the message from the harpy. What does Alonso say? What action do Sebastian and Antonio take? How does Gonzalo interpret their reactions?

7. Explain how Prospero moves his own plans forward in Act 3. Name three ways he uses his magic to control the characters.

Activities & Role-Playing Classes or Informal Groups

Brave Affections Take the roles of Ferdinand, Miranda, and Prospero. Role-play Scene 1, in which Ferdinand and Miranda express their love for each other while Prospero watches their meeting from a distance. Ferdinand is the first man, aside from her father, that Miranda has ever seen. Consider how nervous and excited she is to be accepted by him. Portray Ferdinand's efforts to maintain his honor while performing the menial task of collecting firewood. Research the typical layout of Elizabethan stages and consider where you would position the lovers and the unseen, listening Prospero.

©Shakespeare & Company

Sound and Fury Sound effects and music are an important element in *The Tempest*. Research how Shakespeare's company might have created some of the effects indicated in the stage directions. Then gather samples of music and sound effects that you would use to enhance the play. Search for thunder and lightning, wind, rain, soothing music, barking dogs, and so forth to help the play come alive. Prepare a list to explain how and where you will use each sound.

Discussion   Classes or Informal Groups

1. Review Caliban's lines in Act 2. Do you think he's a "monster"? Why or why not? Has he been treated fairly or unfairly by others on the island?

2. Caliban speaks lines of poetry, but Stephano and Trinculo do not. Because of this, some people believe that Shakespeare intends to show that Caliban has a more noble personality. Do you agree or disagree that speaking in poetry makes Caliban more sympathetic? Why or why not?

3. The harpy suggests that "heart-sorrow / And clear life ensuing" (3.3.95–96) will protect Alonso, Sebastian, and Antonio from the wrath of the gods. What does this mean? How might this lesson fit with Prospero's plans?

4. Study Alonso's reaction after the harpy's departure. Which do you think would be a higher price to pay for past wrongdoings—guilt or punishment? Compare Alonso's reaction to Sebastian and Antonio's response.

Suggestions for Writing   Improve Your Skills

1. In Act 2, Gonzalo described how he would run an imaginary society. Imagine that you are Stephano, getting ready to take over and run the island as your kingdom. Write some notes in preparation for creating your kingdom's laws. What kinds of activities would you encourage among your subjects? What would you forbid?

2. Caliban and Alonso have similar speeches in Act 3. Caliban speaks his in Scene 2 (lines 132–140) and Alonso speaks his in Scene 3 (110–117). Both discuss their feelings about the island's illusions. Write a few sentences describing the images and mood of Caliban's speech; then do the same for Alonso's. What similarities do you notice? What's different? Why?

3. Imagine you are Ferdinand. Stranded on the island, you decide to put a message in a bottle, and throw it into the sea. You hope the tides will carry your story to someone. In your message, write about your emotions when you first washed ashore and your feelings about life on the island near Miranda.

All the World's a Stage Introduction

The Tempest has turned stormy indeed. Prospero's enemies are desperate and wild. Magic, guilt, and despair have driven Alonso, Antonio, and Sebastian to the verge of madness. Meanwhile, Caliban, Trinculo, and Stephano are plotting rape and murder. As the play enters its last acts, audiences might wonder how all this anger and suffering might be resolved. Who will become truly civilized, and who will be ruled by savage emotions?

On one part of the island, however, the mood is much sunnier. There, Ferdinand and Miranda plan to marry. Although far away from Italy, their union would forge a new alliance between Naples and Milan. Will this be the alliance that finally sets things right between Prospero and Alonso?

What's in a Name? Characters

Suppose you had Prospero's powers: magic, knowledge in many branches of science, experience in governing. Would all that talent and experience make you a good ruler?

In *The Tempest,* Prospero seems to pull all the strings. Still, we already know that this godlike man can fail. He takes some of the blame for losing control of his dukedom. Since landing on the island, Prospero has tried to "raise" two characters who grew up there: Miranda and Caliban. Now, Miranda is a virtuous young woman, and Caliban is a violent "wild man." Does this mean that Caliban represents another failure? Prospero doesn't think so. In Act 1, he complained that Caliban's evil "nature" simply could not be improved through kindness and education ("nurture").

In Act 4, we'll see Prospero behaving in ways that are loving and kind, but also angry and strict. Do you feel there is room for improvement in this complex character's nature? Would you like to see Prospero change his ways?

COME WHAT MAY Things to Watch For

Now you see it—and now you don't! Prospero's and Ariel's magic powers often leave the other characters rubbing their eyes in disbelief. Yet Shakespeare's play is much more than a parade of disappearing banquets and sleeping spells. Beyond magic acts, *The Tempest* is about *dreams.*

Watch for how the island's magical environment fits with larger themes of the play. Keep in mind two meanings of the word *illusion.* An illusion can be a simple hallucination or magic trick. Or an illusion can be a belief or a value that is false, such as the love between brothers. Prospero learned this was an illusion when he was betrayed by his brother Alonso. The island is full of both kinds of illusions. They add to the play's dreamlike mood and provide a sense of how quickly life's joys and sorrows can change. Innocence, guilt, anger, love, and forgiveness shift like the magical weather in Shakespeare's romance.

All Our Yesterdays Historical and Social Context

Fire, earth, air, and water. *The Tempest* builds a rich world with the *four elements*. Renaissance scientists believed that they made up all physical matter. In people the four elements were expressed in the *four humours*, fluids that ruled an individual's physical and emotional state.

Fire: *Choler (yellow bile):* Produced by the gall bladder; physical symptoms: heat and dryness; emotional characteristics: violent, revengeful

Earth: *Melancholy (black bile):* Produced by the spleen; physical symptoms: cold and dryness; emotional characteristics: gluttonous, lazy, sentimental

Air: *Blood:* Produced by the liver; physical symptoms: air, heat, and moisture; emotional characteristics: amorous, happy, generous

Water: *Phlegm:* Produced by the lungs; physical symptoms: cold, moisture; emotional characteristics: dull, pale, cowardly

In Act 4, you'll see an example of the theory of the four humours. When Ferdinand discusses his love for Miranda, he talks about "the ardour of my liver." A person who was warm, happy, and loving was ruled by blood. It came from the liver. So a person who was in love was said to be ruled by the liver.

The Play's the Thing Staging

In Act 4, Prospero uses his magic to stage a *masque*. Popular among the wealthy in Shakespeare's day, masques featured beautiful costumes, elaborate stage machinery and scenery, and songs and dances mixed with dialogue. The stories were *allegories*. In an allegory, characters often represent an idea, such as Vice, or a human characteristic, such as Love.

Masques were often performed at court. Often, members of the court, including the royal family, acted in them. If *The Tempest* was first staged at the Blackfriars, its audiences may have been sharp judges of the quality of its masque.

My Words Fly Up Language

In the masque, three characters come from Roman and Greek myth: *Iris*, goddess of the rainbow; *Ceres*, goddess of harvest and crops; and *Juno*, queen goddess of married life. As goddesses of marriage and fertility, their blessing is good luck for Ferdinand and Miranda.

As the masque ends, Prospero's beautiful poetry expresses the play's bittersweet mood. The words *revels, pageant,* and *rack* have a general meaning and also are terms from stage production. Today the most unfamiliar term is *rack*. It means a wisp of high, wind-blown clouds. In the production of a masque, a *rack* was a special effect that made stage clouds seem to dissolve.

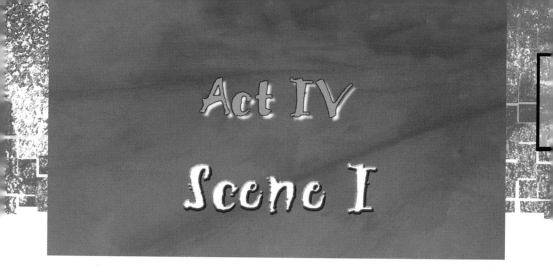

Act IV

Scene I

Before Prospero's Cell. Enter **Prospero, Ferdinand** *and* **Miranda**

Prospero If I have too austerely punished you,
    Your compensation makes amends; for I
    Have given you here a third of mine own life,
    Or that for which I live; who once again
5   I tender to thy hand: all thy vexations
    Were but trials of thy love, and thou
    Hast strangely stood the test: here, afore Heaven,
    I ratify this my rich gift. O Ferdinand,
    Do not smile at me that I boast her off,
10 For thou shalt find she will outstrip all praise,
    And make it halt behind her.

Ferdinand   I do believe it
    Against an oracle.

Prospero Then, as my gift, and thine own acquisition
15 Worthily purchased, take my daughter: but
    If thou dost break her virgin-knot before
    All sanctimonious ceremonies may
    With fully and holy rite be ministered,
    No sweet aspersion shall the heavens let fall
20 To make this contract grow; but barren hate,
    Sour-eyed disdain and discord shall bestrew
    The union of your bed with weeds so loathly
    That you shall hate it both: therefore take heed,
    As Hymen's lamps shall light you.

In front of Prospero's room. **Prospero, Ferdinand,** *and* **Miranda** *enter.*

Prospero If I've punished you too harshly, your compensation makes up for it. I have given you here a third of my own life, or that for which I live. Once again I give her to you. All your trials were just a test of your love. You have stood the test very well. Here before Heaven, I affirm my rich gift to you. Oh Ferdinand, don't smile at me for praising her so highly. You will find that she'll outrun all praise, and make it limp behind her.

Ferdinand I do believe it, even if a prophet said otherwise.

Prospero Then as my gift and your prize, worthily purchased, take my daughter. But if you take her virginity before you are joined in the sacred ceremony of holy matrimony, your marriage will not be watered by the sweet blessings that fall from heaven to make your union grow. Barren hate, sour looks of contempt, and conflict will cover your marriage bed with weeds of loathing, so that you will both hate it. Therefore, take heed, and as you desire happiness in your marriage, let the god of marriage light your way.

25 **Ferdinand**   As I hope
        For quiet days, fair issue and long life,
        With such love as 'tis now, the murkiest den,
        The most opportune place, the strong'st suggestion
        Our worser genius can, shall never melt
30   Mine honour into lust, to take away
        The edge of that day's celebration
        When I shall think, or Phoebus' steeds are foundered,
        Or Night kept chained below.

Prospero   Fairly spoke.
35   Sit, then, and talk with her; she is thine own.
        What, Ariel! My industrious servant, Ariel!

        [*Enter* **Ariel**]

Ariel   What would my potent master? Here I am.

Prospero   Thou and thy meaner fellows your last service
        Did worthily perform; and I must use you
40   In such another trick. Go bring the rabble,
        O'er whom I give thee power, here to this place:
        Incite them to quick motion; for I must
        Bestow upon the eyes of this young couple
        Some vanity of mine Art: it is my promise,
45   And they expect it from me.

Ariel   Presently?

Prospero   Ay, with a twink.

Ariel   Before you can say, 'come' and 'go',
        And breathe twice, and cry, 'so, so',
50   Each one, tripping on his toe,
        Will be here with mop and mow.
        Do you love me, master? No?

Prospero   Dearly, my delicate Ariel. Do not approach
        Till thou dost hear me call.

Ferdinand I hope for quiet days, beautiful children, and a long life with our love just as it is now. Neither the darkest places that offer the most opportunity, nor the strongest temptation of our lower nature can ever melt my honor into lust and take away the enjoyment of our wedding day's celebrations. That day I'll think that the sun's been delayed in its setting, or that night has been kept chained below the horizon and will never come.

Prospero Well said. Sit, then, and talk with her. She is your own. Ariel! My industrious servant, Ariel!

[**Ariel** *enters*]

Ariel What do you want, my powerful master? Here I am.

Prospero You and your lesser spirits worthily performed your last service. Now I must use you in another similar trick. Go and bring here the troop of lesser spirits over whom I've given you power. Urge them to move quickly. I must show this young couple another vision of my magic art. I've promised them, and they expect it from me.

Ariel Right now?

Prospero Yes, in a twinkling.

Ariel Before you can say, "come" and "go," and breathe twice, and cry, "so, so," each one will come here on tiptoe, with grimaces and gestures. Do you love me, master? No?

Prospero Dearly, my delicate Ariel. Don't come here until you hear me call.

55 **Ariel**   Well, I conceive.

                                            [*Exit*]

Prospero Look thou be true; do not give dalliance
         Too much the rein: the strongest oaths are straw
         To th' fire i' th' blood: be more abstemious,
         Or else, good night your vow!

60 **Ferdinand**   I warrant you, sir;
         The white cold virgin snow upon my heart
         Abates the ardour of my liver.

Prospero   Well.
         Now come, my Ariel! Bring a corollary,
65   Rather than want a spirit: appear, and pertly!
         No tongue! All eyes! Be silent.

[*Soft music*]

[*Enter* **Iris**]

Iris *Ceres, most bounteous lady, thy rich leas*
        Of wheat, rye, barley, vetches, oats, and pease;
        Thy turfy mountains, where live nibbling sheep,
70   *And flat meads thatched with stover, them to keep;*
        Thy banks with pioned and twilled brims,
        Which spongy April at thy hest betrims,
        To make cold nymphs chaste crowns; and thy broom-groves,
        Whose shadow the dismissed bachelor loves,
75   *Being lass-lorn; thy poll-clipt vineyard;*
        And thy sea-marge, sterile and rocky-hard,
        Where thou thyself dost air; the queen o' th' sky,
        Whose wat'ry arch and messenger am I,
        Bids thee leave these; and with her sovereign grace,
80   *Here, on this grass-plot, in this very place,*
        To come and sport; her peacocks fly amain:
        Approach, rich Ceres, her to entertain.

Ariel I understand perfectly.

[**Ariel** *exits*]

Prospero [*to* **Ferdinand**] Make sure you're true to your word. Don't get carried away with flirtation. The strongest oaths are like straw to the fire of passion. Stay away from temptation, or else say good night to your vow!

Ferdinand I guarantee, sir, that the snow-white chastity of my beloved cools the heat of my passion.

Prospero Well. Now come, my Ariel! Bring extra spirits. Better too many than too few. Come, and be brisk about it. [*To* **Ferdinand** *and* **Miranda**] No talking! Watch! Be silent!

[*Soft music plays.* **Iris,** *the goddess of the rainbow and the messenger of the gods, enters. She is played by one of the spirits as they perform a masque*]

Iris *Ceres, most bountiful lady, goddess of agriculture, your rich fields of wheat, rye, barley, fodder plants, oats, and peas; your grassy mountains where the nibbling sheep live and flat meadows covered with hay for their keep; your riverbanks thick with twined branches, which moist April at your request trims with flowers to make crowns for chaste virgins; and your groves of shrubs, whose shade the jilted, lovesick bachelor loves; your carefully pruned vineyard; your seashore, bare and rocky-hard, where you yourself walk; queen of the sky, Juno, whose rainbow and messenger I am, requests that you leave these things. Here on this grassy plot, in this very place, come and join in play, with Juno's sovereign grace. Her peacocks who pull her chariot fly swiftly here. Come, rich Ceres, to receive her.*

[*Enter* **Ceres**]

Ceres *Hail, many-coloured messenger, that ne'er*
Dost disobey the wife of Jupiter;
85 *Who, with thy saffron wings, upon my flowers*
Diffusest honey-drops, refreshing showers;
And with each end of thy blue bow dost crown
My bosky acres and my unshrubbed down
Rich scarf to my proud earth, why hath thy queen
90 *Summoned me hither, to this short-grassed green?*

Iris *A contract of true love to celebrate;*
And some donation freely to estate
On the blest lovers.

Ceres   *Tell me, heavenly bow,*
95 *If Venus or her son, as thou dost know,*
Do now attend the queen? Since they did plot
The means that dusky Dis my daughter got,
Her and her blind boy's scandalled company
I have forsworn.

100 **Iris**   *Of her society*
Be not afraid: I met her deity
Cutting the clouds towards Paphos, and her son
Dove-drawn with her. Here thought they to have done
Some wanton charm upon this man and maid,
105 *Whose vows are, that no bed-right shall be paid*
Till Hymen's torch be lighted: but in vain;
Mars's hot minion is returned again;
Her waspish-headed son has broke his arrows,
Swears he will shoot no more, but play with sparrows,
110 *And be a boy right out.*

Ceres   *Highest queen of state,*
Great Juno comes; I know her by her gait.

[*Enter* **Juno**]

[**Ceres** *enters*]

Ceres *Hail, Iris, many-colored messenger, who has never disobeyed Juno, wife of Jupiter; who with your yellow wings upon my flowers sprinkles honey drops, refreshing showers; and with each end of your blue bow crowns my thicket-covered acres and my shrubless downs. Iris, rich scarf of my proud earth, why has your queen summoned me here, to this grassy lawn?*

Iris *To celebrate a contract of true love and to donate something freely from your estate to the blest lovers.*

Ceres *Tell me, heavenly rainbow, do you know if Venus, the love goddess, or her son Cupid still wait upon the Queen? Since that sad day they plotted to help the dark god of the underworld steal my daughter, I've vowed to stay away from her and her blind boy's scandalous company.*

Iris *Don't be afraid of her society. I met her and her son flying through the clouds toward Paphos in a chariot drawn by doves. They thought that they had placed an unchaste spell upon this man and this maid here, who had vowed not to share a bed until they married. But the spell failed. Venus, who is mistress of the god Mars, returned home again. Her irritable son broke all his arrows and swears he won't shoot anymore, but play with sparrows and be a boy again.*

Ceres *Highest queen of state, Great Juno comes. I know her by her royal bearing.*

[**Juno** *enters*]

Juno *How does my bounteous sister? Go with me*
      To bless this twain, that they may prosperous be,
115   *And honoured in their issue.*

            [*Singing*]
            Honour, riches, marriage-blessing,
            Long continuance, and increasing,
            Hourly joys be still upon you!
            Juno sings her blessings on you.

   Ceres   [*Singing*]
120   *Earth's increase, and foison plenty,*
            Barns and garners never empty;
            Vines with clust'ring bunches growing;
            Plants with goodly burthen bowing;
            Spring come to you at the farthest
125   *In the very end of harvest!*
            Scarcity and want shall shun you;
            Ceres' blessing so is on you.

Ferdinand This is a most majestic vision, and
      Harmonious charmingly. May I be bold
130   To think these spirits?

Prospero   Spirits, which by mine Art
      I have from their confines called to enact
      My present fancies.

Ferdinand   Let me liver here ever;
135   So rare a wondered father and a wise
      Makes this place a Paradise.

      [**Juno** and **Ceres** *whisper, and send* **Iris** *on employment*]

Prospero   Sweet, now, silence!
      Juno and Ceres whisper seriously;
      There's something else to do: hush, and be mute,
140   Or else our spell is marred.

Juno *How is my bounteous sister? Go with me to bless these two, that they may be prosperous and honored in their children.*

> *[Singing]*
>> *Honor, riches, marriage-blessing,*
>> *Long continuing, and increasing,*
>> *Hourly joys be always with you!*
>> *Juno sings her blessings on you.*

Ceres *[Singing]*
>> *Earth's abundance, bounties plenty,*
>> *Barns and haylofts never empty;*
>> *Vines with clustering bunches growing;*
>> *Plants with heavy burdens bowing;*
>> *Spring come to you at the farthest*
>> *In the very end of harvest!*
>> *Scarcity and need shall shun you;*
>> *Ceres' blessing so is on you.*

Ferdinand This is a most majestic vision, magically harmonious. Am I correct in thinking that these are spirits?

Prospero Spirits that I have called from their confines by my magic to enact my present fancies.

Ferdinand Let me live here forever. So rare and wise a father-in-law makes this place a paradise.

[**Juno** and **Ceres** *whisper and send* **Iris** *away on a task*]

Prospero Sweet, now, silence! Juno and Ceres whisper seriously. There's something else to do. Hush and be quiet, or else our spell will be broken.

Iris *You nymphs, called Naiads, of the wind'ring brooks,*
With your sedged crowns and ever-harmless looks,
Leave your crisp channels, and on this green land
Answer your summons; Juno does command:
145 *Come, temperate nymphs, and help to celebrate*
A contract of true love; be not too late.

[*Enter certain* **Nymphs**]

You sunburned sicklemen, of August weary,
Come hither from the furrow, and be merry:
Make holiday; your rye-straw hats put on,
150 *And these fresh nymphs encounter every one*
In country footing.

[*Enter certain* **Reapers,** *properly habited. They join with the*
Nymphs *in a graceful dance; towards the end whereof*
Prospero *starts suddenly, and speaks; after which, to a*
strange, hollow, and confused noise, they heavily vanish]

Prospero [*Aside*] I had forgot that foul conspiracy
Of the beast Caliban and his confederates
Against my life: the minute of their plot
155 Is almost come. [*To the* **Spirits**] Well done! Avoid, no more!

Ferdinand This is strange: your father's in some passion
That works him strongly.

Miranda   Never till this day
Saw I him touched with anger, so distempered.

160 **Prospero** You do look, my son, in a moved sort,
As if you were dismayed: be cheerful, sir.
Our revels now are ended. These our actors,
As I foretold you, were all spirits, and
Are melted into air, into thin air:
165 And, like the baseless fabric of this vision,
The cloud-capped towers, the gorgeous palaces,

Iris *You nymphs, called "Naiads," of winding brooks, with your grassy crowns and ever-innocent looks! Leave your rippling brooks and answer your summons on this green land, for so Juno commands. Come, gentle nymphs, and help to celebrate a contract of true love. Do not be late.*

[*Several* **Nymphs** *enter*]

You sunburned reapers, of August weary,
Come here from the furrows and be merry,
Make holiday; your rye-straw hats put on,
And meet these fresh nymphs every one
In country dancing.

[*Several* **Reapers** *enter, properly dressed. They join the* **Nymphs** *in a graceful dance. Toward the end,* **Prospero** *gives a sudden start and speaks. After he speaks, the dancers sorrowfully vanish with a strange, hollow, and confused noise*]

Prospero [*to himself*] I'd forgotten that foul conspiracy of the beast Caliban and his companions against my life. The time of their plot is almost here. [*To the* **Spirits**] Well done! Go on! No more!

Ferdinand This is strange. Your father's very agitated about something.

Miranda Never until this day have I seen him so angry, so out of temper.

Prospero You do look, my son, as if you're upset and worried. Be cheerful, sir. Our revels are over. These actors, as I told you, were all spirits, and are melted into air, into thin air. And like the immaterial contents of this vision, the cloud-capped towers, the gorgeous palaces, the solemn temples—even the

The solemn temples, the great globe itself,
Yea, all which it inherit, shall dissolve,
And, like this insubstantial pageant faded,
170 Leave not a rack behind. We are such stuff
As dreams are made on; and our little life
Is rounded with a sleep. Sir, I am vexed;
Bear with my weakness; my old brain is troubled:
Be not disturbed with my infirmity:
175 If you be pleased, retire into my cell,
And there repose: a turn or two I'll walk,
To still my beating mind.

Ferdinand/Miranda   We wish your peace.

[*Exeunt*]

Prospero Come with a thought. I thank thee: Ariel, come.

[*Enter* **Ariel**]

180 **Ariel** Thy thoughts I cleave to. What's thy pleasure?

Prospero   Spirit,
We must prepare to meet with Caliban.

Ariel Ay, my commander: when I presented Ceres,
I thought to have told thee of it; but I feared
185 Lest I might anger thee.

Prospero Say again, where didst thou leave these varlets?

Ariel I told you, sir, they were red-hot with drinking;
So full of valour that they smote the air
For breathing in their faces; beat the ground
190 For kissing of their feet; yet always bending
Towards their project. Then I beat my tabor;
At which, like unbacked colts, they pricked their ears,
Advanced their eyelids, lifted up their noses
As they smelt music: so I charmed their ears,

great globe of earth itself, and all who inherit it—shall
dissolve, like this insubstantial pageant that has just faded,
leaving not a wisp of cloud behind. We are such stuff as
dreams are made of; and our little life is rounded off with a
sleep. Sir, I am annoyed. Bear with my weakness. My old
brain is troubled. Don't be disturbed by my infirmity. If you
please, retire to my cave, and rest there. I'll walk around a bit
to quiet my unsettled mind.

Ferdinand & Miranda   We wish you peace.

[**Ferdinand** *and* **Miranda** *exit*]

Prospero   I call you with my thought. Thank you, Ariel. Come.

[**Ariel** *enters*]

Ariel   I cling to your thoughts. What's your pleasure?

Prospero   Spirit, we must prepare to meet Caliban.

Ariel   Yes, my commander. When I was acting as Ceres, I
thought I should remind you of it. But I was afraid that you
would be angry.

Prospero   Say again, where did you leave those ruffians?

Ariel   I told you, sir, they were wild with drunkenness. They were
so full of mock courage that they struck the air for breathing in
their faces. They beat the ground for kissing their feet. Yet they
were always moving toward their purpose of killing you. Then
I beat my drum—at which, like unbroken colts, they pricked
their ears, opened their eyelids, and lifted up their noses as
if they smelled the music. So I put a charm on their ears,

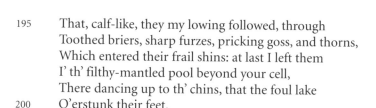

195   That, calf-like, they my lowing followed, through
        Toothed briers, sharp furzes, pricking goss, and thorns,
        Which entered their frail shins: at last I left them
        I' th' filthy-mantled pool beyond your cell,
        There dancing up to th' chins, that the foul lake
200   O'erstunk their feet.

    Prospero   This was well done, my bird.
      Thy shape invisible retain thou still:
      The trumpery in my house, go bring it hither,
      For stale to catch these thieves.

205 **Ariel**   I go, I go.

    Prospero   A devil, a born devil, on whose nature
      Nurture can never stick; on whom my pains,
      Humanely taken, all, all lost, quite lost;
      And as with age his body uglier grows,
210   So his mind cankers. I will plague them all,
      Even to roaring.

    [*Enter* **Ariel,** *loaden with glistering apparel, etc.*]

          Come, hang them on this line.

    [**Prospero** *and* **Ariel** *remain, invisible*]

    [*Enter* **Caliban, Stephano,** *and* **Trinculo,** *all wet*]

    Caliban   Pray you, tread softly, that the blind mole may not
      Hear a foot fall: we now are near his cell.

215 **Stephano**   Monster, your fairy, which you say is a harmless
      fairy, has done little better than played the Jack with us.

    Trinculo   Monster, I do smell all horse-piss; at which my nose
      is in great indignation.

so that, like calves, they followed my music's call through sharp briers, prickly shrubs and gorse, and thorns that pierced their delicate shins. At last I left them in the scummy pool beyond your cave, dancing up and down up to their chins, so that the foul lake stank more than their feet.

Prospero This was well done, my bird. Keep your invisible shape. Go get some cheap finery in my house and bring it here for bait to catch these thieves.

Ariel I go, I go.

[**Ariel** *exits*]

Prospero A devil, a born devil, whose nature can never be changed with teaching; on whom the pains I've humanely taken are lost, all, all lost, quite lost. And just as his body grows uglier with age, so his mind grows more evil. I'll plague them all until they scream in pain.

[**Ariel** *enters, carrying glittering clothing and other items*]

Come, hang them on this line.

[**Prospero** *and* **Ariel** *remain, invisible*]

[**Caliban, Stephano,** *and* **Trinculo** *enter, all wet*]

Caliban Please, walk softly, so that even the blind mole won't hear your footstep. We're now near his cave.

Stephano Monster, your fairy—which you say is a harmless fairy—has done little better than played tricks on us.

Trinculo Monster, I smell like horse urine, which greatly bothers my nose.

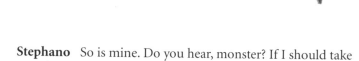

Stephano So is mine. Do you hear, monster? If I should take
220   a displeasure against you, look you –

Trinculo Thou wert but a lost monster.

Caliban Good my lord, give me thy favour still.
        Be patient, for the prize I'll bring thee to
        Shall hoodwink this mischance: therefore speak softly.
225   All's hushed as midnight yet.

Trinculo Ay, but to lose our bottles in the pool!

Stephano There is not only disgrace and dishonour in that,
        monster, but an infinite loss.

Trinculo That's more to me than my wetting: yet this is your
230   harmless fairy, monster.

Stephano I will fetch off my bottle, though I be o'er ears for
        my labour.

Caliban Prithee, my King, be quiet. See'st thou here,
        This is the mouth o' th' cell: no noise, and enter.
235   Do that good mischief which may make this island
        Thine own for ever, and I, thy Caliban,
        For aye thy foot-licker.

Stephano Give me thy hand. I do begin to have bloody
        thoughts.

240 **Trinculo** O King Stephano! O peer! O worthy Stephano!
        Look what a wardrobe here is for thee!

Caliban Let it alone, thou fool; it is but trash.

Trinculo O, ho, monster! We know what belongs to a
        frippery. O King Stephano!

245 **Stephano** Put off that gown, Trinculo; by this hand, I'll have
        that gown.

Trinculo Thy grace shall have it.

Stephano Mine too. Do you hear, monster? If I should take displeasure with you, watch out—

Trinculo You'd be a lost monster.

Caliban My good lord, don't turn against me. Be patient, for the prize I'll bring you to will make you blind to this misfortune. So speak softly. All's as hushed as midnight.

Trinculo Yes, but to lose our bottles in that pool!

Stephano There's not only disgrace and dishonor in that, monster, but also an infinite loss.

Trinculo That means more to me than my getting wet. But this is your "harmless" fairy, monster.

Stephano I'll fetch my bottle, even if I'm buried in filth for my trouble.

Caliban Please, my king, be quiet. See here, this is the mouth of his cave. No noise, now. Enter. Do that good mischief that will make this island your own forever, and I, your Caliban, forever your foot-licker.

Stephano Give me your hand. I'm beginning to have bloody thoughts.

Trinculo Oh King Stephano! Oh peer! Oh worthy Stephano! Look what a wardrobe is here for you!

Caliban Let it alone, you fool. It's just trash.

Trinculo Oh, ho, monster! We know what belongs in a second-hand clothes shop. Oh King Stephano!

Stephano Take off that gown, Trinculo. By my hand, I'll have that gown.

Trinculo Your Grace shall have it.

Caliban   The dropsy drown this fool! What do you mean
To dote thus on such luggage? Let't alone,
250   And do the murder first: if he awake,
From toe to crown he'll fill our skins with pinches,
Make us strange stuff.

Stephano   Be you quiet, monster. Mistress line, is not this my
jerkin? Now is the jerkin under the line: now, jerkin, you are
255   like to lose your hair, and prove a bald jerkin.

Trinculo   Do, do; we steal by line and level, an't like your
grace.

Stephano   I thank thee for that jest; here's a garment for't: wit
shall not go unrewarded while I am King of this country.
260   'Steal by line and level' is an excellent pass of pate; there's
another garment for't.

Trinculo   Monster, come, put some lime upon your fingers,
and away with the rest.

Caliban   I will have none on't: we shall lose our time,
265   And all be turned to barnacles, or to apes
With foreheads villainous low.

Stephano   Monster, lay-to your fingers: help to bear this away
where my hogshead of wine is, or I'll turn you out of my
kingdom: go to, carry this.

270   **Trinculo**   And this.

Stephano   Ay, and this.

[*A noise of hunters is heard. Enter divers* **Spirits,** *in shape of
dogs and hounds, hunting them about;* **Prospero** *and* **Ariel**
set them on]

Prospero   Hey, Mountain, hey!

Ariel   Silver! there it goes, Silver!

Caliban May this fool drown! What do you mean by fawning over such stuff? Let it alone and do the murder first. If he wakes up, he'll fill our skins with pinches from head to toe, and make strange stuff of us.

Stephano Be quiet, you monster. Madam Line, isn't this the jacket for me! But this jacket is not a quality line. Now jacket, you are likely to lose your hair and become a bald jacket.

Trinculo Bravo! We'll steal by plumb line and level, like professionals, if it please Your Grace.

Stephano I thank you for that joke. Here's a garment for it. Wit will not go unrewarded while I am king of this country. "Steal by plumb line and level" is an excellent joke. There's another garment for it.

Trinculo Monster, come, put something sticky on your fingers and steal the rest.

Caliban I'll have none of it. We lose our chance, and we'll all be turned to geese or apes with wretchedly low foreheads.

Stephano Monster, get your fingers working. Help carry this away to where my barrel of wine is, or I'll turn you out of my kingdom. Go on. Carry this.

Trinculo And this.

Stephano Yes, and this.

[*A noise of hunters is heard. Several* **Spirits** *enter in the shapes of dogs and hounds. They chase* **Stephano, Trinculo,** *and* **Caliban. Prospero** *and* **Ariel** *urge them on*]

Prospero Hey, Mountain, hey!

Ariel Silver! There it goes, Silver!

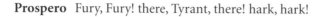

Prospero Fury, Fury! there, Tyrant, there! hark, hark!

[**Caliban, Stephano** *and* **Trinculo** *are driven out*]

275 Go charge my goblins that they grind their joints
With dry convulsions; shorten up their sinews
With aged cramps; and more pinch-spotted make them
Than pard or cat o' mountain.

Ariel   Hark, they roar!

280 **Prospero** Let them be hunted soundly. At this hour
Lies at my mercy all mine enemies:
Shortly shall all my labours end, and thou
Shalt have the air at freedom: for a little
Follow, and do me sevice.

[*Exeunt*]

Prospero Fury, Fury! There, Tyrant, there! Hark, hark!

[**Caliban, Stephano,** *and* **Trinculo** *are driven away*]

Go order my goblins to grind their joints with convulsions. Tighten their muscles with cramps such as old people have, and pinch them until they are more spotted than leopards or wildcats.

Ariel Listen how they roar!

Prospero Let them be hounded thoroughly. At this hour, all my enemies are at my mercy. Shortly all my labors will end, and you shall breathe the air of freedom. For just a little longer, follow me and do me a service.

[**Prospero** *and* **Ariel** *exit*]

Comprehension Check What You Know

1. Why was Prospero "testing" Ferdinand before Act 4?

2. What promise does Ferdinand make to Prospero in Scene 1?

3. Name the goddesses that Prospero asks to show his magical powers to Ferdinand and Miranda. What things or states do these goddesses watch over?

4. Prospero interrupts the masque and sends the spirits away in anger. Why is he angry?

5. Ariel has been making trouble for Stephano, Trinculo, and Caliban. What does Ariel report to Prospero about how he led these plotters astray?

6. What do Stephano and Trinculo find on the way to Prospero's cell that causes them to delay carrying out their scheme? How does Caliban react to their discovery?

7. Prospero and Ariel are secretly watching Stephano, Trinculo, and Caliban. At the end of Act 4, how does Prospero punish them for their evil plan?

Activities & Role-Playing Classes or Informal Groups

The Magic Clothesline Take the roles of Prospero, Ariel, Caliban, Stephano, and Trinculo. Role-play the second half of Scene 1, after Ferdinand and Miranda have exited. Imagine Stephano and Trinculo as they strut around in

©Shakespeare & Company

their newfound clothes. Consider Caliban's anxiousness to carry on with their plan. Consider that Prospero is on to their plot. How does this affect the mood of the scene? Are the characters' actions suspenseful or comedic?

World of Illusion Act 4 features some amazing sights. With the masque, Shakespeare even gives us a kind of play-within-a-play. There are many such moments in Shakespeare's works. He also frequently uses language that includes theatrical double-meanings. Review Scene 1, lines 35–55 and from line

146 to the end. Make a list of any lines or words you think could refer to special effects, acting, or other theatrical illusions. How do you think this type of language and imagery contributes to the play's mood? In what ways is Prospero similar to a stage director or writer as he watches over the island?

Discussion Classes or Informal Groups

1. Review the following lines by Prospero regarding Caliban in Act 4. What does Prospero mean? Do you agree with his words?

   A devil, a born devil, on whose nature
   Nurture can never stick; on whom my pains,
   Humanely taken, all, all lost, quite lost;
   And as with age his body uglier grows,
   So his mind cankers.

2. At the end of Act 4, Prospero says he has all his enemies at his mercy. Referring to Act 4 only, describe two ways in which Prospero has shown his power. Has he used it for good purposes? Who might resent this power?

3. What aspects of married life are symbolized by the images and speakers in the masque? What kind of marriage does Prospero want for his daughter?

Suggestions for Writing Improve Your Skills

1. Caliban and Ariel are both servants of Prospero, and yet they are different. Write two paragraphs that compare and contrast them. Then add a paragraph explaining how you might cast and costume these characters. Explain your choices.

2. Review the lines or poetic images from Scene 1 and write a prose sentence for each that explains what the line describes: "Which spongy April at thy hest betrims" (4.1.72), "Rich scarf to my proud earth" (4.1.89), "cloud-capped towers" (4.1.166), and "our little life / Is rounded with a sleep" (4.1.171–2). For each line, add a sentence explaining why you think Shakespeare might have chosen these images.

3. Imagine you are Ariel. In a few short hours you will be free—no longer Prospero's slave. You will need to find a job suitable for a spirit. Write a résumé for a future employer in which you describe your good qualities. Include a list of your past work experiences and add some suggestions for how you will assist your next employer.

All the World's a Stage Introduction

How will things sort out? As things stand, life on the island seems hard and confused. Act 4 ended on a note of dark justice as the magic hounds chased Stephano, Trinculo, and Caliban. Prospero was in a vengeful mood. Only Miranda and Ferdinand felt happy. If any of the other characters are to leave the island with a feeling of peace, magic must work some powerful changes. Some wounds must heal, and some wrongdoers must repent.

What's in a Name? Characters

Many people have noticed similarities between Prospero and Shakespeare. Often Prospero's magic involves staging "shows" for others, such as the masque. Does Prospero direct and create the play's action through his "Art"? Could Prospero's need to get everything done in three hours be compared to a playwright's need to shape his plot for a play?

In Act 5, we'll watch Prospero complete his work of magic art. As you read, consider how you feel about this character. He is powerful and fascinating but not always likeable. Has he changed? How? Is he prepared to give up his powers and return to Italy? Do you think he'll be a better ruler for Milan than he was before?

COME WHAT MAY Things to Watch For

In Act 5, watch for how characters both look back and look forward. For some, it's a time of wonder and awe. Miranda, for example, sees the beginnings of a "brave new world" ahead of her. Others may find it harder to let go of the past.

Have you ever looked back on past difficulties and decided they had some positive aspects? In *The Tempest,* this learning experience may be related to the common Renaissance Christian notion of a "fortunate fall." It stated that the "fall" from Eden and humankind's later suffering led to the glorious outcome of Christian redemption. Some characters may interpret the difficult events of the day as evidence of the actions of a wiser power. Have you noticed similar ideas working elsewhere in the play?

All Our Yesterdays Historical and Social Context

Prospero is an example of a *magus*. His sorcery is very different from the type practiced by Sycorax, Caliban's mother. In Shakespeare's time, a magus was believed to be a kind of respectable witch. For the magus, magic and the occult were serious areas of scholarly investigation. His powers grew from study and knowledge.

The Play's the Thing Staging

In Act 5 Prospero finally "discovers," or reveals, Ferdinand and Miranda as they sit playing chess. Most scholars believe this means Prospero opens a door or curtain to show the couple inside a small "discovery space" on stage. This area probably was also used for Prospero's "cell," or cave.

Shakespeare's audience was very conscious of how an actor's costume helped identify his role in the play and indicate symbolic meanings. As you read Act 5, watch for an important costume change by Prospero. What might this simple action tell you about his character at this point in the play?

My Words Fly Up Language

The final speech in *The Tempest* is called an *epilogue*. An epilogue was a traditional speech made by an actor to signal the end of the play and to ask the audience for applause. Because many readers think that Prospero is a stand-in for Shakespeare himself, they interpret *The Tempest's* epilogue as Shakespeare's farewell to his life on the stage. Others reject this idea, arguing that the epilogue is not great poetry and may not have been written by Shakespeare at all!

Silence sometimes speaks almost as loudly as words. As you read Act 5, pay attention to who does *not* speak. Specifically, notice how little is said by Antonio, a very important character in the play. Why do you think Shakespeare keeps him quiet here?

Act V

Scene I

Before the Cell of Prospero. Enter **Prospero** *in his magic robes, and* **Ariel**

Prospero Now does my project gather to a head:
    My charms crack not; my spirits obey; and time
    Goes upright with his carriage. How's the day?

Ariel On the sixth hour; at which time, my lord,
5   You said our work should cease.

Prospero   I did say so,
    When first I raised the tempest. Say, my spirit,
    How fares the King and 's followers?

Ariel   Confined together
10   In the same fashion as you gave in charge,
    Just as you left them; all prisoners, sir,
    In the lime-grove which weather-fends your cell;
    They cannot budge till your release. The King,
    His brother, and yours, abide all three distracted,
15   And the remainder mourning over them,
    Brimful of sorrow and dismay; but chiefly
    Him you termed, sir, 'The good old lord, Gonzalo';
    His tears run down his beard, like winter's drops
    From eaves of reeds. Your charm so strongly works 'em,
20   That if you now beheld them, your affections
    Would become tender.

In front of Prospero's cell. **Prospero** *enters in his magic robes, followed by* **Ariel**.

Prospero Now my project is coming to a head. My charms have not broken; my spirits obey. And Time, whose burdens are now lightened as my work nears completion, can walk upright. What's the time of day?

Ariel It's six o'clock, the time, my lord, that you said our work would be finished.

Prospero I did say that when I first raised the tempest. Say, my spirit, how are the king and his followers?

Ariel They're kept together in the manner that you instructed, just as you left them. They're all prisoners, sir, in the lime-grove that shields your cell from the weather. They cannot budge until you release them. The king, his brother, and your brother are all three in a state of distraction. The rest are mourning over them, brimful of sorrow and dismay, especially the one you called, sir, "The good old lord, Gonzalo." His tears run down his beard, like winter's raindrops from the eaves of a thatched roof. Your charm is working on them so strongly that if you saw them now, your feelings would soften.

Prospero   Dost thou think so, spirit?

Ariel Mine would, sir, were I human.

Prospero   And mine shall.

25   Hast thou, which art but air, a touch, a feeling
       Of their afflictions, and shall not myself,
       One of their kind, that relish all as sharply,
       Passion as they, be kindlier moved than thou art?
       Though with their high wrongs I am struck to th' quick,

30   Yet with my nobler reason 'gainst my fury
       Do I take part: the rarer action is
       In virtue than in vengeance: they being penitent,
       The sole drift of my purpose doth extend
       Not a frown further. Go release them, Ariel:
35   My charms I'll break, their senses I'll restore,
       And they shall be themselves.

Ariel   I'll fetch them, sir.

                                   [*Exit*]

Prospero Ye elves of hills, brooks, standing lakes, and groves;
       And ye that on the sands with printless foot
40   Do chase the ebbing Neptune, and do fly him
       When he comes back; you demi-puppets that
       By moonshine do the green sour ringlets make,
       Whereof the ewe not bites; and you whose pastime
       Is to make midnight mushrooms, that rejoice
45   To hear the solemn curfew; by whose aid –
       Weak masters though ye be – I have bedimmed

       The noontide sun, called forth the mutinous winds,
       And 'twixt the green sea and the azured vault
       Set roaring war: to the dread rattling thunder
50   Have I given fire, and rifted Jove's stout oak
       With his own bolt; the strong-based promontory
       Have I made shake, and by the spurs plucked up
       The pine and cedar: graves at my command

Prospero Do you think so, spirit?

Ariel Mine would, sir, if I were human.

Prospero And mine will. You, who are just air, have a touch, a feeling for their sufferings. Then shouldn't I myself, one of their kind, who feels everything just as sharply as they feel it, be more moved than you are? Though I'm struck to the quick by their high wrongs against me, I take the side of my reason, my nobler quality, against my anger. The more virtuous act is forgiveness rather than vengeance. Since they are repentant, then my purpose is achieved. Go release them, Ariel. I'll break my charms and restore their senses, and they'll be themselves again.

Ariel I'll fetch them, sir.

[**Ariel** *exits*]

Prospero You elves of hills, brooks, quiet lakes, and groves! And you who, with foot so light it leaves no print on the sands, chase Neptune, god of the ocean, as he ebbs, and flee from him when he comes back. You fairies, who by the moonshine make your fairy rings in the grass, which the ewe will not eat. And you, whose pastime is to make the mushrooms grow at midnight, who rejoice to hear the solemn curfew bell. With your aid—although you're less powerful demons—I've dimmed the noontime sun, summoned the mutinous winds, set the green sea and the blue vault of the sky at war with each other. I've given fire to the dreaded roar of thunder and split the oak—the god Jove's sacred tree—with his own thunderbolt. I've shaken the solid land that juts out over the sea, and plucked up the pine and cedar trees by their roots. By my powerful art, at my command graves have wakened those sleeping in them,

55 Have waked their sleepers, oped, and let 'em forth
By my so potent Art. But this rough magic
I here abjure; and, when I have required
Some heavenly music – which even now I do –
To work mine end upon their senses, that
This airy charm is for, I'll break my staff,

60 Bury it certain fathoms in the earth,
And deeper than did ever plummet sound
I'll drown my book.

[*Solemn music*]

[*Here enters* **Ariel** *before: then* **Alonso,** *with a frantic gesture attended by* **Gonzalo; Sebastian** *and* **Antonio** *in like manner, attended by* **Adrian** *and* **Francisco.** *They all enter the circle which* **Prospero** *had made, and there stand charmed; which* **Prospero** *observing, speaks:*]

A solemn air, and the best comforter
To an unsettled fancy, cure thy brains,
65 Now useless, boiled within thy skull! There stand,
For you are spell-stopped.
Holy Gonzalo, honourable man,
Mine eyes, ev'n sociable to the show of thine,
Fall fellowly drops. The charm dissolves apace;
70 And as the morning steals upon the night,
Melting the darkness, so their rising senses
Begin to chase the ignorant fumes that mantle
Their clearer reason. O good Gonzalo,
My true preserver, and a loyal sir
75 To him thou follow'st! I will pay thy graces
Home both in word and deed. Most cruelly
Didst thou, Alonso, use me and my daughter:
Thy brother was a furtherer in the act.
Thou art pinched for't now, Sebastian. Flesh and blood,
80 You, brother mine, that entertained ambition,

opened, and let them out. But I here renounce this rough
magic. And when I have needed some heavenly music—
which I do even now—to work my charms upon the senses
of those whom this sweet music is for, I'll break my wand in
half, bury it in the earth at a certain depth, and drown my
book in the ocean, deeper than has ever been measured.

[*Solemn music.* **Ariel** *enters, followed by* **Alonso** *gesturing
frantically, attended by* **Gonzalo**; **Sebastian** *and* **Antonio** *enter
in the same condition, attended by* **Adrian** *and* **Francisco**.
They all enter the magic circle which **Prospero** *has made and
stand there under his spell. Observing,* **Prospero** *speaks.*]

Let this solemn music, the best comforter for an unsettled
mind, cure your brains, which are useless now in your skull!
Stand there, for you are spell-bound. Saintly Gonzalo,
honorable man, my eyes shed teardrops in sympathy with
yours. The charm is fading quickly. And as the morning
creeps upon the night, melting away the darkness, so their
awakening senses begin to chase away the clouds that hide
the clearness of their mind. O good Gonzalo, my true
lifesaver, and a loyal gentleman to the man you follow. I'll
reward your services in full, both in word and in deed.
Alonso, you abused me and my daughter most cruelly. Your
brother was an accomplice in the act. You are caught in the
truth now, Sebastian. You, my brother, my flesh and blood,
who gave in to ambition; who refused to feel remorse and

Expelled remorse and nature; whom, with Sebastian –
Whose inward pinches therefore are most strong –
Would here have killed your King; I do forgive thee,
Unnatural though thou art. Their understanding
85   Begins to swell; and the approaching tide
Will shortly fill the reasonable shore,
That now lies foul and muddy. Not one of them
That yet looks on me, or would know me: Ariel,
Fetch me the hat and rapier in my cell:
90   I will discase me, and myself present
As I was sometime Milan: quickly, spirit;
Thou shalt ere long be free.

[**Ariel** *sings and helps to attire him*]

> *Where the bee sucks, there suck I;*
> *In a cowslip's bell I lie;*
95   *There I couch when owls do cry.*
> *On the bat's back I do fly*
> *After summer merrily.*
> *Merrily, merrily shall I live now*
> *Under the blossom that hangs on the bough.*

100 **Prospero** Why, that's my dainty Ariel! I shall miss thee;
But yet thou shalt have freedom: so, so, so.
To the King's ship, invisible as thou art:
There shalt thou find the mariners asleep
Under the hatches; the master and the boatswain
105   Being awake, enforce them to this place,
And presently, I prithee.

  Ariel I drink the air before me, and return
Or ere your pulse twice beat.

  Gonzalo All torment, trouble, wonder and amazement
110   Inhabits here: some heavenly power guide us
Out of this fearful country!

natural affection of brother for brother; and who, with Sebastian—whose guilt therefore is strongest—would have killed your king here. I do forgive you, unnatural though you are. Their understanding is beginning to return like a flood, and the approaching tide of reason will soon wash over their minds, which are now foul and muddy. Not one of them can see me yet, or would know me if he could. Ariel, fetch me the hat and dagger in my cell. I'll take off these magician's robes and dress myself as I was before—the Duke of Milan. Quickly, spirit. You'll be free before long.

[**Ariel** *sings and helps to dress* **Prospero**]

Where the bee sucks, there suck I;
In a cowslip's bell I lie;
There I sleep when owls do cry.
On the bat's back I do fly
After summer merrily.
Merrily, merrily shall I live now
Under the blossom that hangs on the bough.

Prospero Why that's my dainty Ariel! I'll miss you. But you will have your freedom. So, so, so. Go to the king's ship. Remain invisible. There you'll find the sailors asleep below deck. When the captain and the boatswain awaken, bring them to this place, and quickly, if you please.

Ariel I'll fly quickly through the air and return before your pulse beats twice.

[**Ariel** *exits*]

Gonzalo This place is filled with torment, trouble, wonder, and amazement. May some heavenly power guide us out of this fearful country!

Prospero   Behold, Sir King,
The wronged Duke of Milan, Prospero:
For more assurance that a living Prince
115   Does now speak to thee, I embrace thy body;
And to thee and thy company I bid
A hearty welcome.

Alonso   Whether thou be'st he or no,
Or some enchanted trifle to abuse me,
120   As late I have been, I not know: thy pulse
Beats, as of flesh and blood; and, since I saw thee,
Th' affliction of my mind amends, with which,
I fear, a madness held me: this must crave –
An if this be at all – a most strange story.
125   Thy dukedom I resign, and do entreat
Thou pardon me my wrongs. But how should Prospero
Be living and be here?

Prospero   First, noble friend
Let me embrace thine age, whose honour cannot
130   Be measured or confined.

Gonzalo   Whether this be
Or be not, I'll not swear.

Prospero   You do yet taste
Some subtleties o' the isle, that will not let you
135   Believe things certain. Welcome, my friends all!
[*Aside to* **Sebastian** *and* **Antonio**] But you, my brace of lords,
                                were I so minded,
I here could pluck his highness' frown upon you,
And justify you traitors: at this time
140   I will tell no tales.

Sebastian [*Aside*]   The devil speaks in him.

Prospero Behold, Sir King, the wronged Duke of Milan, Prospero. To assure you that a living prince, and not a spirit, is speaking to you, I embrace your body. And to you and your company I bid a hearty welcome.

Alonso Whether you're Prospero or not, or some enchanted trick to abuse me, as has happened lately, I don't know. Your pulse beats, like flesh and blood. And since I saw you, the affliction of my mind is cured, which was, I fear, a kind of madness. If this is really happening, it must have a most remarkable explanation. I resign your dukedom, and I beg you to pardon me my wrongdoings. But how can Prospero be living and be here?

Prospero First, noble friend, let me embrace your revered self, whose honor is immeasurable and limitless.

Gonzalo Whether this is real or not real, I can't swear to.

Prospero You still taste the illusions of this island, which will not let you believe the things that are real. Welcome, all my friends! [*Aside to* **Sebastian** *and* **Antonio**] But you, my pair of lords, if I had a mind to, I could bring his highness's wrath upon you, and prove you to be traitors. But for the time being, I'll tell no tales.

Sebastian [*Aside*] The devil speaks through him.

Prospero   No.
For you, most wicked sir, whom to call brother
Would even infect my mouth, I do forgive
145 Thy rankest fault – all of them; and require
My dukedom of thee, which perforce, I know,
Thou must restore.

Alonso   If thou be'st Prospero,
Give us particulars of thy preservation;
150 How thou hast met us here, whom three hours since
Were wracked upon this shore; where I have lost –
How sharp the point of this remembrance is! –
My dear son Ferdinand.

Prospero   I am woe for't, sir.

155 **Alonso** Irreparable is the loss; and patience
Says it is past her cure.

Prospero   I rather think
You have not sought her help, of whose soft grace
For the like loss I have her sovereign aid,
160 And rest myself content.

Alonso   You the like loss!

Prospero As great to me, as late; and, supportable
To make the dear loss, have I means much weaker
Than you may call to comfort you, for I
165 Have lost my daughter.

Alonso   A daughter?
O heavens, that they were living both in Naples,
The King and Queen there! That they were, I wish
Myself were muddled in that oozy bed
170 Where my son lies. When did you lose your daughter?

Prospero In this last tempest. I perceive, these lords
At this encounter do so much admire,
That they devour their reason, and scarce think
Their eyes do offices of truth, their words
175 Are natural breath: but, howsoe'er you have
Been justled from your senses, know for certain

Prospero No. As for you, wicked sir. To call you brother would poison my mouth. But I do forgive your most awful deed—no all of them. And I demand my dukedom from you, which I know by necessity you must return to me.

Alonso If you're Prospero, give us the details of how you were saved. Tell us how you met us here, who three hours ago were wrecked upon this shore, where I lost—how sharply painful this memory is!—my dear son Ferdinand.

Prospero I'm sorry for that, sir.

Alonso The loss is irreparable. Even patience cannot cure the pain.

Prospero I think you have not sought the help of patience. By her mercy, I received her aid for a similar loss, and I am now at peace.

Alonso You had a similar loss?

Prospero As great to me, and as recently. And to make the loss bearable, I have much less to comfort me than you have. I have lost my daughter.

Alonso A daughter? Oh heavens! I wish that they were both living in Naples, as the king and queen there! I would wish myself lying in the mud of that oozy bed where my son lies, if only they both were in Naples. When did you lose your daughter?

Prospero In this last tempest. I see that these lords' mouths gape open in astonishment. They can't believe what they see. They're unable to speak. But no matter how shocked you are, you can be certain that I am Prospero. I'm the same

That I am Prospero, and that very duke
Which was thrust forth of Milan; who most strangely
Upon this shore, where you were wracked, was landed,
180   To be the lord on't. No more yet of this;
For 'tis a chronicle of day by day,
Not a relation for a breakfast, nor
Befitting this first meeting. Welcome, sir;
This cell's my court: here have I few attendants,
185   And subjects none abroad: pray you, look in.
My dukedom since you have given me again,
I will requite you with as good a thing;
At least bring forth a wonder, to content ye
As much as me my dukedom.

[*Here* **Prospero** *discovers* **Ferdinand** *and* **Miranda** *playing
at chess*]

190 **Miranda** Sweet lord, you play me false.

Ferdinand   No, my dearest love,
I would not for the world.

Miranda Yes, for a score of kingdoms you should wrangle,
And I would call it fair play.

195 **Alonso**   If this prove
A vision of the island, one dear son
Shall I twice lose.

Sebastian   A most high miracle!

Ferdinand Though the seas threaten, they are merciful;
200   I have cursed them without cause.

Alonso   Now all the blessings
Of a glad father compass thee about!
Arise, and say how thou cam'st here.

duke who was sent away from Milan, the same person who, in such a strange manner, landed upon this shore and became the lord of the island where you were shipwrecked. No more of this now. It's a story that will take days to tell, not one for telling over breakfast or suitable for this first meeting. Welcome sir. This cell's my court. I have few attendants here, and no subjects anywhere on this island. Please, look in. Since you've given me my dukedom again, I'll repay you with something just as good, or at least bring forth something wonderful, to please you as much as my dukedom pleases me.

[**Prospero** *shows them* **Ferdinand** *and* **Miranda** *playing chess inside*]

Miranda   Sweet lord, you are cheating.

Ferdinand   No, my dearest love, I would not for the world.

Miranda   Yes, of course, you should do so for the *world.* In fact, you should try to win for nothing more than twenty kingdoms. I would call it fair.

Alonso   If this turns out to be an illusion of this island, I'll have lost one dear son twice.

Sebastian   A most high miracle!

Ferdinand   Though the seas are threatening, they are merciful. I have cursed them without cause.

Alonso   Now all the blessings of a happy father surround you! Arise, and tell me how you came to be here.

Miranda O, wonder!
205 How many goodly creatures are there here!
How beauteous mankind is! O brave new world,
That has such people in it!

Prospero 'Tis new to thee.

Alonso What is this maid with whom thou wast at play?
210 Your eld'st acquaintance cannot be three hours:
Is she the goddess that hath severed us,
And brought us thus together?

Ferdinand Sir, she is mortal;
But by immortal Providence she's mine:
215 I chose her when I could not ask my father
For his advice, nor thought I had one. She
Is daughter to this famous Duke of Milan,
Of whom so often I have heard renown,
But never saw before; of whom I have
220 Received a second life; and second father
This lady makes him to me.

Alonso I am hers:
But, O, how oddly will it sound that I
Must ask my child forgiveness!

225 **Prospero** There, sir, stop:
Let us not burthen our remembrances with
A heaviness that's gone.

Gonzalo I have inly wept,
Or should have spoke ere this. Look down, you gods,
230 And on this couple drop a blessed crown!
For it is you that have chalked forth the way
Which brought us hither.

Alonso I say, Amen, Gonzalo!

Gonzalo Was Milan thrust from Milan, that his issue
235 Should become Kings of Naples? O, rejoice
Beyond a common joy! And set it down

Miranda Oh, what a wonder! How many fine creatures there are here! How beautiful mankind is! Oh brave new world, that has such people in it!

Prospero It's new to you.

Alonso Who is this maid with whom you were playing chess? You could not have known her for more than three hours. Is she the goddess that separated us and brought us back together?

Ferdinand Sir, she is mortal. But by immortal Providence she's mine. I chose her when I couldn't ask my father for his advice—when I didn't think I had a father. She is daughter to this famous duke of Milan of whom I had so often heard praised but had never seen, and of whom I've received a second life, and a second father—which this lady makes him to me.

Alonso I am her father as well. But, oh, how odd it will sound for me to ask my child for forgiveness!

Prospero There, sir, stop. Let's not burden ourselves with reminders of a sorrow that has passed.

Gonzalo I've been weeping inwardly, or I would have spoken before now. Look down, you gods, and drop a blessed crown on this couple! For it is you that have shown the way that brought us here.

Alonso I say, amen, Gonzalo!

Gonzalo Was the duke of Milan cast out of Milan so that his descendants should become kings of Naples? Oh, rejoice, beyond all common joys! And write it down in gold on stone

With gold on lasting pillars: in one voyage
Did Claribel her husband find at Tunis;
And Ferdinand, her brother, found a wife
240   Where he himself was lost; Prospero his dukedom
In a poor isle; and all of us ourselves
When no man was his own.

Alonso   [*To* **Ferdinand** *and* **Miranda**] Give me your hands:
Let grief and sorrow still embrace his heart
245   That doth not wish you joy!

Gonzalo   Be it so! Amen!

[*Enter* **Ariel** *with the* **Master** *and* **Boatswain** *amazedly
following*]

O, look, sir, look, sir! Here is more of us:
I prophesied, if a gallows were on land,
This fellow could not drown. Now, blasphemy,
250   That swear'st grace o'erboard, not an oath on shore?
Hast thou no mouth by land? What is the news?

Boatswain   The best news is, that we have safely found
Our King, and company; the next, our ship –
Which, but three glasses since, we gave out split –
255   Is tight and yare and bravely rigged, as when
We first put out to sea.

Ariel   [*Aside to* **Prospero**] Sir, all this service
Have I done since I went.

Prospero   [*Aside to* **Ariel**] My tricksy spirit!

260   **Alonso**   These are not natural events; they strengthen
From strange to stranger. Say, how came you hither?

Boatswain   If I did think, sir, I were well awake,
I'd strive to tell you. We were dead of sleep,
And – how we know not – all clapped under hatches;
265   Where, but even now, with strange and several noises

pillars: in one voyage Claribel found her husband at Tunis, and Ferdinand, her brother, found a wife, when he himself was lost; Prospero found his dukedom in this poor island; and all of us found ourselves when no man was in his right mind.

Alonso [*To* **Ferdinand** *and* **Miranda**] Give me your hands. If anyone does not wish you joy, let grief and sorrow fill his heart forever.

Gonzalo Let it be so! Amen!

[**Ariel** *enters with the* **Captain** *and* **Boatswain***, both in a state of amazement*]

Oh, look sir! Look, sir! Here are more of us. I prophesied that as long as a gallows stood on land, this fellow could not drown. Now, you blasphemer, whose swearing drove grace overboard, don't you have an oath on shore? Now that you're on land, don't you have a mouth? What's the news?

Boatswain The best news is that we have safely found our king and company. The next is that our ship—which just three hours ago we said was wrecked—is watertight, trim, and finely rigged, just as it was when we first put out to sea.

Ariel [*Aside to* **Prospero**] Sir, I've done all this service since I last left here.

Prospero [*Aside to* **Ariel**] My spritely, smart spirit!

Alonso These are not natural events. They get stranger and stranger. Say, how did you come here?

Boatswain If I thought I were fully awake, sir, I'd try to tell you. We were in a dead sleep, and—how we don't know—all locked below deck. Then, just now, we were awakened with strange noises of different kinds—roaring, shrieking,

Of roaring, shrieking, howling, jingling chains,
And more diversity of sounds, all horrible,
We were awaked; straightway, at liberty;
Where we, in all our trim, freshly beheld
270 Our royal, good, and gallant ship; our master
Cap'ring to eye her: on a trice, so please you,
Even in a dream, were we divided from them,
And were brought moping hither.

Ariel [*Aside to* **Prospero**]   Was't well done?

275 **Prospero** [*Aside to* **Ariel**] Bravely, my diligence. Thou shalt
be free.

Alonso This is as strange a maze as e'er men trod;
And there is in this business more than nature
Was ever conduct of: some oracle
280 Must rectify our knowledge.

Prospero   Sir, my liege,
Do not infest your mind with beating on
The strangeness of this business; at picked leisure
Which shall be shortly single, I'll resolve you,
285 Which to you shall seem probable, of every
These happened accidents; till when, be cheerful,
And think of each thing well. [*Aside to* **Ariel**] Come hither,
     spirit:
Set Caliban and his companions free;
290 Untie the spell. [*Exit* **Ariel**] How fares my gracious sir?
There are yet missing of your company
Some few odd lads that you remember not.

[*Enter* **Ariel,** *driving in* **Caliban, Stephano,** *and* **Trinculo,**
in their stolen apparel]

Stephano Every man shift for all the rest, and let no man
take care for himself; for all is but fortune. Coragio, bully-
295 monster, coragio!

howling, jingling chains, and other kinds of sounds, all horrible. Then suddenly we were no longer below deck. We were free and well. Then we saw our royal, good, and gallant ship. Our captain was jumping for joy to see her. And in a split second, as if in a dream, we were separated from the others and brought here in confusion.

Ariel [*Aside to* **Prospero**] Was this done well?

Prospero [*Aside to* **Ariel**] Excellent, my diligent servant. You shall be free.

Alonso This is as strange a maze as ever a man tried to find his way through. And there's more in this business than nature could be responsible for. Some oracle must help us understand this.

Prospero Sir, my sovereign, don't trouble your mind with worrying about the strangeness of this business. At a convenient moment, which shall be shortly, I myself will explain everything that has happened and answer your questions as clearly as I can. Until then, be cheerful, and be assured that everything is fine. [*Aside to* **Ariel**] Come here, spirit. Set Caliban and his companions free. Untie the spell. [**Ariel** *exits*] How are you, my gracious sir? There are still some of your company missing, a few lads unaccounted for, that you don't remember.

[**Ariel** *enters, driving in* **Caliban, Stephano,** *and* **Trinculo,** *wearing their stolen clothing.*]

Stephano Let every man shift for all the rest, and let no man take care of himself. All is just luck. Courage, bully-monster, courage!

Trinculo If these be true spies which I wear in my head,
here's a goodly sight.

Caliban O Setebos, these be brave spirits indeed!
How fine my master is! I am afraid
300 He will chastise me.

Sebastian   Ha, ha!
What things are these, my lord Antonio?
Will money buy 'em?

Antonio   Very like; one of them
305 Is a plain fish, and, no doubt, marketable.

Prospero Mark but the badges of these men, my lords,
Then say if they be true. This mis-shapen knave,
His mother was a witch; and one so strong
That could control the moon, make flows and ebbs,
310 And deal in her command, without her power.
These three have robbed me; and this demi-devil –
For he's a bastard one – had plotted with them
To take my life. Two of these fellows you
Must know and own; this thing of darkness I
315 Acknowledge mine.

Caliban   I shall be pinched to death.

Alonso Is not this Stephano, my drunken butler?

Sebastian He is drunk now: where had he wine?

Alonso And Trinculo is reeling ripe: where should they
320 Find this grand liquor that hath gilded 'em?
How cam'st thou in this pickle?

Trinculo I have been in such a pickle, since I saw you last,
that, I fear me, will never out of my bones: I shall not fear
fly-blowing.

325 **Sebastian** Why, how now, Stephano!

Stephano O, touch me not; I am not Stephano, but a cramp.

Trinculo If I can trust these eyes in my head, then here's a welcome sight.

Caliban Oh, devil Setebos, these are wonderful spirits indeed! How finely dressed my master is! I'm afraid he'll punish me.

Sebastian Ha, ha! What are these things, my lord Antonio? Will money buy them?

Antonio Very likely. One of them is a plain fish, and no doubt, marketable.

Prospero Look at the clothes these men wear, my lords, then say if they're honest. This misshapen knave, his mother was a witch. She was so strong that she could control the moon, make the tides flow and ebb, and act with the moon's authority. These three have robbed me. And this half-devil— he's an ill-begotten one—plotted with them to take my life. You must know and own two of these fellows. This thing of darkness I acknowledge as mine.

Caliban I'll be pinched to death.

Alonso Isn't this Stephano, my drunken butler?

Sebastian He's drunk now. Where did he get the wine?

Alonso And Trinculo is reeling drunk. Where could they have found this grand liquor that has made them so drunk that their faces are flushed? How did you get in such a pickle?

Trinculo I've been so pickled since I saw you last that I'm afraid I'll never get it out of my bones. I'm so well preserved I'll never fear flies.

Sebastian Why, hello, Stephano!

Stephano Oh, don't touch me! I'm not Stephano, I'm one big cramp.

Prospero You'd be King o' the isle, sirrah?

Stephano I should have been a sore one, then.

Alonso This is a strange thing as e'er I looked on. [*Pointing to* **Caliban**]

330 **Prospero** He is as disproportioned in his manners
As in his shape. Go, sirrah, to my cell;
Take with you your companions; as you look
To have my pardon, trim it handsomely.

Caliban Ay, that I will; and I'll be wise hereafter,
335 And seek for grace. What a thrice-doubled ass
Was I, to take this drunkard for a god,
And worship this dull fool!

Prospero   Go to; away!

Alonso Hence, and bestow your luggage where you found it.

340 **Sebastian** Or stole it, rather.

[*Exeunt* **Caliban, Stephano** *and* **Trinculo**]

Prospero Sir, I invite your Highness and your train
To my poor cell, where you shall take your rest
For this one night; which, part of it, I'll waste
With such discourse as, I not doubt, shall make it
345 Go quick away: the story of my life,
And the particular accidents gone by
Since I came to this isle: and in the morn
I'll bring you to your ship, and so to Naples,
Where I have hope to see the nuptial
350 Of these our dear-beloved solemnized;
And thence retire me to my Milan, where
Every third thought shall be my grave.

Alonso   I long
To hear the story of your life, which must
355 Take the ear strangely.

Prospero So, you'd be king of this island, you knave?

Stephano I'd have been a sore one, then.

Alonso This is the strangest thing I've ever seen. [*pointing to* **Caliban**]

Prospero He's as warped in his manners as he is in his shape. Go, scoundrel, to my cell. Take your companions with you. If you want to have my pardon, then be well behaved.

Caliban Aye, that I will. And I'll be wise from now on, and seek your blessing. What a thrice-double ass I was, to take this drunkard for a god, and worship this stupid fool!

Prospero Go on, now. Away!

Alonso Go, and return your stuff you carry where you found it.

Sebastian Or stole it, rather.

[**Caliban, Stephano,** *and* **Trinculo** *exit*]

Prospero Sir, I invite Your Highness and your attendants to my poor cell, where you can take your rest for this one night. I'll spend part of this night in talk that, I don't doubt, will make the night go quickly. I'll tell the story of my life and the particular details that have happened since I came to this island. In the morning I'll bring you to your ship. And then to Naples, where I hope to see the wedding vows of these dear beloveds solemnized. After that I'll retire to Milan, where every third thought will be about my grave.

Alonso I long to hear the story of your life, which no doubt will hold my attention.

Prospero   I'll deliver all;
And promise you calm seas, auspicious gales,
And sail so expeditious, that shall catch
Your royal fleet far off. [*Aside to* **Ariel**] My Ariel, chick,
360   That is thy charge: then to the elements
Be free, and fare thou well! Please you, draw near.

[*Exeunt*]

Epilogue *spoken by* **Prospero**

Now my charms are all o'erthrown,
And what strength I have's mine own,
Which is most faint: not, 'tis true,
365   *I must be here confined by you,*
Or sent to Naples. Let me not,
Since I have my dukedom got,
And pardoned the deceiver, dwell
In this bare island by your spell;
370   *But release me from my bands*
With the help of your good hands:
Gentle breath of yours my sails
Must fill, or else my project fails,
Which was to please. Now I want
375   *Spirits to enforce, Art to enchant;*
And my ending is despair,
Unless I be relieved by prayer,
Which pierces so, that it assaults
Mercy itself, and frees all faults.
380   *As you from crimes would pardoned be,*
Let your indulgence set me free.

[*Exit*]

Prospero I'll tell you everything. And I promise you calm seas, pleasant winds, and a voyage so swift that you'll catch your royal fleet, even though it's far off. [*aside to* **Ariel**] My Ariel, chick, that is your job. Then, to the air be free, and fare you well! [*To the audience*] If you please, come with me.

[*Exit all but* **Prospero**]

Epilogue *spoken by* **Prospero**
>   *My magic charms are all overthrown.*
>   *What strength I have is just my own,*
>   *And that's most weak. Now, it's true*
>   *I must here be kept by you*
>   *Or sent to Naples. Let me not —*
>   *Since I have my dukedom got,*
>   *And pardoned the deceiver—dwell*
>   *In this bare island by your spell.*
>   *But release me from my bands*
>   *With the help of your good hands*
>   *Clapping. Their gentle breeze my sails*
>   *Must fill, or else my project fails,*
>   *Which was to please. Now I want*
>   *Spirits to enforce, Art to enchant*
>   *And my ending is despair,*
>   *Unless I'm helped out by a prayer*
>   *So powerful that it assaults*
>   *Mercy itself, and frees my faults.*
>   *As you from crimes would pardoned be,*
>   *Let your applause then set me free.*

[**Prospero** *exits*]

Comprehension   Check What You Know

1. How does Ariel suggest Prospero treat his enemies?

2. In Act 5, what does Prospero decide to give up?

3. When Prospero appears before Alonso, Gonzalo, Sebastian, and Antonio, he whispers a warning to Sebastian and Antonio. What does he threaten to tell Alonso about Sebastian and Antonio?

4. What does Prospero demand of his brother Sebastian?

5. Sebastian exclaims "a most high miracle!" What miracle do Alonso, Gonzalo, Sebastian, and Antonio witness?

6. According to the Boatswain, what is the condition of the ship following the storm?

7. Caliban, Stephano, and Trinculo are brought in front of all the men. Where does Prospero send them?

Activities & Role-Playing   Classes or Informal Groups

Reconciliation Take the roles of Prospero, Ariel, Alonso, Gonzalo, Sebastian, Antonio, Miranda, and Ferdinand. Role-play Act 5 starting from the point in which Ariel brings Alonso, Gonzalo, Sebastian, and Antonio before Prospero and stopping at the point in which Ariel returns with the Boatswain and Master. How does each man react to seeing Prospero after so many years? Imagine how they react when they see Ferdinand, who was thought to have drowned during the storm.

Louis A. Lotorto as Ariel in The Shakespeare Theater's 1989 production of *The Tempest* directed by Richard E. T. White. Photo by Joan Marcus.

Lightness and Darkness Make a list describing how you would light the stage for Act 5. Keep in mind all the activity that occurs, as well as the mood. How will you light the scene in which Prospero speaks to the circle of men while they are under his spell? Will the lights be brighter—or darker—when they are released from the spell? The men are amazed when Prospero shows them Miranda and Ferdinand playing chess. Would you use any special lighting to enhance this part of the scene? How would you light the epilogue?

Discussion Classes or Informal Groups

1. Study the following lines by Prospero. Discuss the meaning of the lines.

   Yet with my nobler reason 'gainst my fury
   Do I take part: the rarer action is
   In virtue than in vengeance

2. Prospero forgives all of the men for their "high wrongs." Does each man deserve Prospero's forgiveness? Does Alonso deserve forgiveness more than Sebastian? Is Sebastian as guilty as Antonio and Alonso?

3. Review the epilogue. Discuss the meaning behind Prospero's final words.

Suggestions for Writing Improve Your Skills

1. Select three of the main characters and choose a quote for each that best summarizes their personality. Explain your reasoning for selecting each quote.

2. Imagine you are Prospero. You have just arrived in Italy after a long journey from the island and you are eager to record your experiences. Write a chapter from your autobiography describing the events that brought about your return to your rightful role as Duke of Milan. Describe how you were transformed from a man seeking vengeance to a man offering forgiveness.

The Tempest
Additional Resources

Books

Title: *The Riverside Shakespeare*
Author: J. J. M. Tobin et al. (editor)
Publisher: Houghton Mifflin
Year: 1997
Summary: This volume features all of Shakespeare's plays along with 40 pages of color and black-and-white plates. In addition, each play has a scholarly introduction and individual commentary. The book also contains general background material on the Shakespearean stage and Elizabethan history.

Title: *The Complete Works of Shakespeare*
Author: David Bevington (editor)
Publisher: Addison-Wesley Publishing Company
Year: 1997
Summary: This book offers the complete, unabridged works of Shakespeare as edited by the current president of the Shakespeare Association of America. Editor David Bevington also provides an introductory essay for each play and a general introduction to Shakespeare's life, times, and stage.

Title: *Shakespeare: A Life*
Author: Park Honan
Publisher: Oxford University Press
Year: 1999
Summary: Using the little available data that exists, Honan pieces together this biographical account of Shakespeare's life.

Title: *A Shakespeare Glossary*
Author: C. T. Onions (editor)
Publisher: Oxford University Press
Year: 1986
Summary: This classic reference book defines all of the now-obscure words used by Shakespeare in his plays and shows how the meaning of words that are still common may have changed. The book provides examples and gives play locations for the words.

Title: *Shakespeare A to Z: The Essential Reference to His Plays, His Poems, His Life and Times, and More*
Author: Charles Boyce
Publisher: Facts on File
Year: 1990
Summary: This book features over 3,000 encyclopedic entries arranged alphabetically. It covers several areas of Shakespeare, including historical background, play synopses, entries for individual characters, and critical commentary.

Title: *The Shakespearean Stage: 1574–1642*
Author: Andrew Gurr
Publisher: Cambridge University Press
Year: 1992 (3rd edition)
Summary: An overview of Shakespearean staging by Andrew Gurr, one of the foremost experts in this area. The book highlights the many different theater companies of the day and how they performed.

Title: *Shakespeare's Book of Insults, Insights & Infinite Jests*
Author: John W. Seder (editor)
Publisher: Templegate
Year: 1984
Summary: This entertaining book covers several categories of jabs and mockeries taken straight from the text of Shakespeare's plays.

Title: *The Meaning of Shakespeare* (2 volumes)
Author: Harold Goddard
Publisher: University of Chicago Press
Year: 1960
Summary: Originally published in 1951, this classic, hefty work of Shakespearean criticism includes essays on all of Shakespeare's plays. (Note: Since Goddard's work is in two volumes, readers who seek information on particular plays should make sure they obtain the volume containing commentary on that play.)

Title: *The Tempest: A Guide to the Play*
Author: Herbert R. Coursen
Publisher: Greenwood Publishing Group
Year: 2000
Summary: A comprehensive overview of the play, its sources, and historical and cultural contexts.

Title: *The Tempest*
Author: Sandra Clark
Publisher: Penguin Critical Studies
Year: 1999
Summary: A strong, balanced review of the play, its themes, characters, and general critical analysis.

Videos

Title: *The Plays of William Shakespeare: The Tempest*
Director: William Woodman
Year: 1992
Summary: A very clear and understandable production of Shakespeare's play. Starring Efrem Zimbalist, Jr., William H. Bassett, Ted Sorel, and Ron Palillo.

Title: *Tempest*
Director: Paul Mazursky
Year: 1982
Summary: A loose adaptation of Shakespeare's play, updated to modern times and starring John Cassavetes and Gena Rowlands.

Title: *The Tempest*
Director: Derek Jarman
Year: 1979
Summary: A low-budget and visually imaginative adaptation of the play.

Title: *Forbidden Planet*
Director: Fred M. Wilcox
Year: 1956
Summary: A "pop," classical science-fiction adaptation of Shakespeare's play.

Audiotapes

Title: *The Tempest*
Producer: Harper Audio
Year: 1996
Summary: An abridged version of the play.

Title: *The Tempest*
Producer: Arkangel Shakespeare
Year: 2000
Summary: A full-length version of the play, presented in a dramatic-reading format.

Title: *All the World's a Stage: An Anthology of Shakespearian Speeches Performed by the World's Leading Actors*
Producer: BBC Radio
Year: 1995
Summary: A collection of some of the finest performances of Shakespeare's famous passages. Laurence Olivier, Richard Burton, and Vanessa Redgrave are featured, along with several other notable actors.

Web Sites

URL: *www.rdg.ac.uk/globe/research/research_index.htm*
Summary: Associated with The Globe Theatre's web site, this collection of research links offers information on the building and rebuilding of The Globe, Shakespeare's relationship to the theatre, and miscellaneous articles on theatrical traditions and practices during Shakespeare's time.

URL: *www.tech-two.mit.edu/Shakespeare/hamlet/index.html*
Summary: MIT's Shakespeare web site; offers full texts of the
plays in a searchable format.

URL: *http://daphne.palomar.edu/Shakespeare/*
Summary: "Mr. William Shakespeare and the Internet" offers
a wide variety of links to other Shakespeare sites.
"Criticism," "Educational," and "Life & Times" are just a
few of the categories offered.

Software

Title: *Shakespeare Trivia*
Developer: Cascoly Software
Grades: All
Platform: Windows
Summary: A trivia game for any ability or knowledge level.
Test your knowledge of Shakespeare. The program
includes 37 plays, over 1,200 characters, over 400 scenes,
and 500 individual quotes. Allows the player to choose the
level of difficulty and type of question.

Title: *Shakespeare's Language*
Developer: Randal Robinson and Peter Holben Wehr
Grades: 9–12, College
Platform: Mac
Summary: This program helps a reader identify, classify, and
respond to causes of difficulty in Shakespeare's language.
It helps the reader work effectively with syntactical diffi-
culties, unfamiliar words, figurative language, unexpected
and multiple meanings of words, and special connotations
of words.

Notes

Notes